Knit and Crochet for Small Dolls

Marjory Fainges

Dedication

I dedicate this book to all the doll collectors, young and old, who love their small dolls, whether they be modern, collectible or antique.

First edition/First printing

To purchase additional copies of this book, please contact:
Reverie Publishing Company, 130 South Wineow Street, Cumberland, MD 21502
888-721-4999 • www.reveriepublishing.com

Library of Congress Control Number 2007923109

ISBN 978-1-932485-47-9

Project Editor: Krystyna Poray Goddu
Design and Production: Tammy S. Blank

Front cover, clockwise from left: 2006 Mary Englebreit's Ann Estelle by the Tonner Doll Company; 2006 model by the Alexander Doll Company; 2006 Ginny by the Vogue Doll Company; 1980s reproduction of a German celluloid doll; 2006 Riley by Kish & Company; 1940s Patsy look-a-like; 2005 model by Heidi Plusczok.

Back cover: Riley by Kish & Company (full view); 2006 model by the Alexander Doll Company (head shot).

Printed and bound in Korea

Knit and Crochet for Small Dolls

Marjory Fainges

Acknowledgements

I wish to extend my sincere thanks to the late Evelyn Jane Coleman, who was responsible for me furthering my research into the history of knitted and crocheted dolls' clothing, leading me to design clothes suitable for assorted dolls, especially in keeping with their period of manufacture.

A very special thanks to the following American companies: Tonner Doll Company, Lawton Doll Company, Kish & Company, Vogue Doll Company and Alexander Doll Company, all of which graciously supplied me with dolls that I could use as mannequins to show off the various outfits in this book. My thanks also to those who encouraged me in writing this book, especially my husband Jim and my daughter Lyn, who provided very useful and helpful constructive criticism.

Introduction

During the past sixteen years I have had published several books on knitting and crocheting for dolls as small as 3 inches to those as tall as 22 inches, using a variety of yarns, and sizes of knitting needles and crochet hooks. Over these years I have been studying the type of clothing that has been made for dolls from as far back as the 1890s, particularly the knitted and crocheted patterns that were commercially published, enabling people to make a wide range of clothing for various types of dolls in their own homes. I have found that very little has been published commercially in recent years for dolls ranging in size from 6 to 9 inches, except for the plethora of patterns that were published in the 1950s and 1960s for teen dolls (almost worldwide at that time). Recognizing the new-found growing popularity for dolls in this smaller size range, I decided it was time to sit down and see what I could come up with in regard to new patterns. I found it quite challenging, but also very rewarding, particularly when the garment I was working on was finished. I hope you have the same experience in completing the patterns in this book.

To show the extensive variety of dolls that can wear the clothes in this book, I have used a wide range of different models. A great number of manufacturers have made, and still do make, dolls in this size range. In the past these included Ideal, Vogue and Alexander; today both Vogue and Alexander continue to produce small dolls, in addition to contemporary manufacturers such as Kish & Company, Tonner Doll Company, Lawton Doll Company and Raikes Collectibles. Quite a few of the patterns in this book will also fit, and are ideal for, many of the small hard-plastic dolls that were produced in massive numbers elsewhere in the world, and sold under trade names such as Pedigree, Rosebud, Roddy and Amanda Jane. The patterns should fit a number of small antique dolls, as well as contemporary artist dolls and some imported mass-produced china dolls made in Asian countries.

Whatever dolls we own—be they travel dolls, flea-market finds, play dolls for our children or fine pieces for display only, we all like our dolls to be dressed. I hope the garments in this book may help fulfill that need.

Contents

Notes on the Patterns

American terminology has been used throughout the book, whether the patterns are in knitting or crochet, as well as the sizes, gauges, etc. for both knitting needles and crochet hooks. All measurements are given in inches, followed by metric measurements.

The sizes, gauges, etc., for the knitted articles were made using the Knit-Chek metal gauge created by Susan Bates of Chester, Connecticut. For the steel (aluminium) crochet hooks, I have used the sizes listed in the American edition of *The Ultimate Source Book of Knitting and Crochet Stitches* published by Reader's Digest.

Where possible, well-known American yarns have been used, such as: DMC No. 8 Perle cotton, DMC No. 20 or DMC Cebelia No. 20 crochet cotton, DMC Babylo 10 or DMC Cebelia No. 10 (equal to 3 ply), DMC Petra No. 5 or DMC Perle No. 5, etc. (equal to 4 ply).

Some of the garments have also been made using Cameo yarns (equal to 2 ply), an American yarn normally used in punch embroidery, and their equivalents. Note that the DMC No. 8 Perle cotton is slightly finer than many of the other imported No. 8 Pearl cottons now available, so if you choose to use a different No. 8 Pearl cotton, which gives a softer texture to the finished garment, be sure to allow for a possible slight difference in the size of the finished pattern. I have also used other yarns, such as 4 ply soft knitting cotton sold worldwide, including those manufactured by Sullivan or the Coats/Milford/Semco conglomerate. I have made many of the patterns in two yarns, and given the different sizes and tensions used in the making of said garments in order to provide readers with an even greater variety of garments.

Classification of Patterns

I have classified each pattern according to level of difficulty, as follows.

*Easy: These patterns are good for beginners, and more experienced workers can often complete one in an evening

**Moderate: Knitters and crocheters of average ability may confidently undertake these patterns.

***Advanced: Some experience is needed to complete these patterns, which also take more time, but are well worth the effort.

For the garments included within this book, I have worked using only a small range of both knitting needles and crochet hooks. If you wish to make some of these clothes for larger or smaller dolls, it is simply a question of using larger or smaller knitting needles or crochet hooks and changing the ply, or denier, of the yarn used. This adaptation has proved very successful by those who have used my patterns in the other knitting and crochet books for dolls that have been published over the past ten or so years.

Knitting Needles Sizes
#0 US - 2 mm (14 Imperial)
#1 US - 2.25 mm (13 Imperial)
#2 US - 2.75 mm (12 Imperial)

Steel Crochet Hook Sizes
#8 US - 1.25 mm
#7 US - 1.5 mm
#4 US - 1.75 mm
#1 US - 2 mm

Although these are steel crochet hook sizes, you can often buy these crochet hooks in coated aluminum, which I have found easier to use. If you are a loose knitter or crocheter, it is very important that you use a crochet hook or knitting needles one size smaller than specified. If you are a tight knitter or crocheter, use a larger crochet hook or knitting needles.

Terminology and Abbreviations

Many of the following terms apply to both knitting and crocheting.

*	repeat instructions between * and *
***	refer back to previous section of pattern
#	number, when used in conjunction with knitting needle or hook size
alt	alternate
beg	begin/beginning
CC or **CC1**	contrasting color, used when working with more than one color
cast off	bind off
ch	chain in crochet
cm	centimeter
dc	double crochet (same as tr or treble in some countries)
2 dc tog	2 double crochets worked together as a way to decrease a stitch
dec	decrease (work two stitches together to form one stitch)
garter st	work every row in knit stitch
hdc	half double crochet (same as htr or half treble in some countries)
in	inches
inc	increase (work twice into next stitch)
inc3 or **M3**	increase by knitting into the front of the stitch, then back of the stitch and then in front of stitch, thus making three stitches from one stitch
k	knit
k2 tog	knitting 2 stitches together to form one stitch (used in decreasing)
m1 or **yoh**	make a stitch by placing yarn over needle before the next stitch
MC	main color, when working with more than one color
mm	millimeter
miss	skip a stitch
ms	moss stitch or seed stitch, usually worked with an uneven number of stitches, k1, p1, alternately along row, to create a broken rib effect
no	number

p	purl
pt or **picot**	work 3 or 4 ch, then join, by working into 1st stitch of the 3rd or 4th ch
psso	pass the slipped stitch over a stitch that has previously been knitted
p2sso	pass the two stitches that have just been slipped over a stitch that has been knitted
rep	repeat
rib	k1, p1, worked on an even number of stitches, and repeated to end of row
rnd	round
sc	single crochet (same as dc or double crochet in some countries)
shell or **sh.**	in crochet, work 3 or 5 dc into the same st
snap	snap fastener (press-studs in some countries)
sl. or **sl st**	in knitting, slip stitch from one knitting needle to the other
sl. or **sl st**	in crochet, working into stitch, and pulling thread straight through, thus not making a stitch, but being able to work along a row to a certain point
st/s	stitch/s
st. st	stocking or stockingnette stitch: knit row, followed by a purl row
tog	working two stitches together to form one stitch
turn	reverse the way of knitting by working back on the needle just worked
undershirt	singlet or undervest in some countries
wl bk	when knitting a purl row, bring yarn to back of needle before working next stitch
wl fwd	bring yarn to front of work before working next stitch, thus making a stitch
wrn	bring the wool over and around the needle
wyt	weave your thread when using two colors or for knitting a border of a contrast color to the garment, weave the color yarn you are about to knit under or over the color just used, and when you make the next st, just give a gentle pull on the color you are not using

The Models and Their Measurements

Alexander Doll Company 2006 models

Height	8 inches	20 cm
Shoulder to sole of foot	5½ inches	14 cm
Shoulder to waist	1½ inches	4 cm
Underarm to waist	½ inch	1 cm
Width around at underarm	4½ inches	11.5 cm
Width around at waist	4¾ inches	12 cm
Arm (underarm to wrist)	1¼ inches	3 cm
Waist to crotch	1½ inches	4 cm
Waist to ankle	3¾ inches	9.5 cm
Inside leg (crotch to ankle)	2¼ inches	6 cm
Width around head (above eyes)	6 inches	15 cm

Betsy McCall, Dru & Mary Englebreit's Ann Estelle: Tonner Doll Company 2006 models

Height	8 inches	20 cm
Shoulder to sole of foot	5¾ inches	14.5 cm
Shoulder to waist	1½ inches	4 cm
Underarm to waist	½ inch	1 cm
Width around at underarm	3¾ inches	9.5 cm
Width around at waist	3¾ inches	9.5 cm
Arm (underarm to wrist)	1¼ inches	3 cm
Waist to crotch	1¾ inches	4.5 cm
Waist to ankle	4 inches	10 cm
Inside leg (crotch to ankle)	2½ inches	6.5 cm
Width around head	5½ inches	14 cm

Ginny: Vogue Doll Company 2006 vintage reproduction model & 1950s hard-plastic model

(Note: the contemporary Vogue Ginny is 8 inches high, ½-inch higher than the 1950s doll and the contemporary vintage Ginny model.)

Height	7½ inches	19 cm
Shoulder to sole of foot	5½ inches	14 cm
Shoulder to waist	1½ inches	4 cm
Underarm to waist	¾ inch	2 cm
Width around at underarm	4¼ inches	11 cm
Width around at waist	4¼ inches	11 cm
Arm (underarm to wrist)	1½ inches	4 cm
Waist to crotch	1½ inches	4 cm
Waist to ankle	3½ inches	4 cm
Inside leg (crotch to ankle)	2 inches	5 cm
Width around head	6 inches	15 cm

Riley: Kish & Company 2006 model

Height	7½ inches	19 cm
Shoulder to sole of foot	5¾ inches	14.5 cm
Shoulder to waist	1½ inches	4 cm
Underarm to waist	¾ inch	2 cm
Width around at underarm	4 inches	10 cm
Width around at waist	4¼ inches	11 cm
Arm (underarm to wrist)	1½ inches	4 cm
Waist to crotch	2 inches (front)	5 cm
	1½ inches (back)	4 cm
Waist to ankle	4 inches	10 cm
Inside leg (crotch to ankle)	2½ inches	6.5 cm
Width around head	5 inches	12.5 cm

Heidi Plusczok 2005 model

Height	8½ inches	22 cm
Shoulder to sole of foot	7 inches	18 cm
Shoulder to waist	2 inches	5 cm
Underarm to waist	¾ inch	2 cm
Width around at underarm	5 inches	12.5 cm
Width around at waist	5 inches	12.5 cm
Arm (underarm to wrist)	1¾ inches	4.5 cm
Waist to crotch	1¾ inches	4.5 cm
Waist to ankle	4½ inches	11.5 cm
Inside leg (crotch to ankle)	2¾ inches	7 cm
Width around head	5½ inches	14 cm

Lightly Lily & Katrena (2002 UFDC Souvenir): Lawton Doll Company 2002 & 2006 models

Height	9 inches	22.5 cm
Shoulder to sole of foot	6½ inches	16.5 cm
Shoulder to waist	1½ inches	4 cm
Underarm to waist	½ inch	1 cm
Width around at underarm	4¼ inches	11 cm
Width around at waist	4 inches	10 cm
Arm (underarm to wrist)	2 inches	5 cm
Waist to crotch	2 inches	5 cm
Waist to ankle	4½ inches	11.5 cm
Inside leg (crotch to ankle)	2¾ inches	7 cm
Width around head	6 inches	15 cm

Hitty: Raikes Collectibles 2002 model

Height	6½ inches	16.5 cm
Shoulder to sole of foot	5¼ inches	13.5 cm
Shoulder to waist	1¼ inches	3 cm
Underarm to waist	½ inch	1.5 cm
Arm (underarm to wrist)	1½ inches	4 cm
Width around at underarm	4 inches	10 cm
Width around at waist	4 inches	10 cm
Waist to crotch	1½ inches	4 cm
Waist to ankle	3½ inches	9 cm
Inside leg (crotch to ankle)	2 inches	5 cm
Width around head	4 inches	10 cm

Wooden Doll: Raikes Collectibles 2002 model

Height	9 inches	23 cm
Shoulder to sole of foot	7¼ inches	18.5 cm
Shoulder to waist	1¾ inches	4.5 cm
Underarm to waist	¾ inch	2 cm
Arm (underarm to wrist)	1¾ inches	4.5 cm
Width around at underarm	4¼ inches	11 cm
Width around at waist	4 inches	10 cm
Waist to crotch	1¾ inches	4.5 cm
Waist to ankle	5 inches	13 cm
Inside leg (crotch to ankle)	3½ inches	9 cm
Width around head	5½ inches	14 cm

Modern China Doll: 1990s model made in China

Height	7½ inches	19 cm
Shoulder to sole of foot	6½ inches	16.5 cm
Shoulder to waist	1¾ inches	4.5 cm
Underarm to waist	½ inch	1.5 cm
Arm (underarm to wrist)	1¼ inches	3 cm
Width around at underarm	4 inches	10 cm
Width around at waist	3½ inches	9 cm
Waist to crotch	1¼ inches	3 cm
Waist to ankle	4 inches	10 cm
Inside leg (crotch to ankle)	2½ inches	6.5 cm
Width around head	4½ inches	11.5 cm

Celluloid Doll Reproduction: 1980s model by an unknown German maker

Height	8 inches	20 cm
Shoulder to sole of foot	6½ inches	16.5 cm
Shoulder to waist	1¾ inches	4.5 cm
Underarm to waist	¾ inch	2 cm
Arm (underarm to wrist)	1¾ inches	4.5 cm
Width around at underarm	4½ inches	11.5 cm
Width around at waist	4½ inches	11.5 cm
Waist to crotch	1¾ inches	4.5 cm
Waist to ankle	4½ inches	11.5 cm
Inside leg (crotch to ankle)	2¾ inches	7 cm
Width around head	5¾ inches	14.5 cm

Amanda Jane: Amanda Jane Doll Company circa-1979 model

Height	7½ inches	19 cm
Shoulder to sole of foot	6 inches	15 cm
Shoulder to waist	1¾ inches	4.5 cm
Underarm to waist	¾ inch	2 cm
Arm (underarm to wrist)	1½ inches	4 cm
Width around at underarm	3½ inches	9 cm
Width around at waist	3¼ inches	8.5 cm
Waist to crotch	1¼ inches	3 cm
Waist to ankle	3½ inches	9 cm
Inside leg (crotch to ankle)	2½ inches	6.5 cm
Width around head	4½ inches	11.5 cm

Miss Curity type: 1960s/1970s model by unknown maker

Height	7½ inches	19 cm
Shoulder to sole of foot	5¾ inches	14.5 cm
Shoulder to waist	1½ inches	4 cm
Underarm to waist	¾ inch	2 cm
Arm (underarm to wrist)	1¼ inches	3 cm
Width around at underarm	4 inches	10 cm
Width around at waist	3¾ inches	9.5 cm
Waist to crotch	1¼ inches	3 cm
Waist to ankle	3½ inches	9 cm
Inside leg (crotch to ankle)	2¼ inches	6 cm
Width around head	4¾ inches	12 cm

Patch: Pedigree 1960s model

(Note: This doll is similar to the Ideal Company's Pepper, Tammy's little sister, of the same era.)

Height	9 inches	22.5 cm
Shoulder to sole of foot	6¾ inches	17 cm
Shoulder to waist	1¾ inches	4.5 cm
Underarm to waist	¾ inch	2 cm
Width around at underarm	4¼ inches	11 cm
Width around at waist	3¾ inches	9.5 cm
Arm (underarm to wrist)	1¾ inches	4.5 cm
Waist to crotch	1½ inches	4 cm
Waist to ankle	4¾ inches	12 cm
Inside leg (crotch to ankle)	3 inches	7.5 cm
Width around head	5½ inches	14 cm

Patsy Look-a-like: 1940s model by an unknown maker

Height	8½ inches	21.5 cm
Shoulder to sole of foot	6½ inches	16.5 cm
Shoulder to waist	1¾ inches	4.5 cm
Underarm to waist	¾ inch	2 cm
Width around at underarm	5¼ inches	13 cm
Width around at waist	5½ inches	14 cm
Arm (underarm to wrist)	1¼ inches	3 cm
Waist to crotch	1¾ inches	4.5 cm
Waist to ankle	4½ inches	11.5 cm
Inside leg (crotch to ankle)	2¾ inches	7 cm
Width around head	6¾ inches	17 cm

K*R/Halbig: circa-1910 model

Height	7½ inches	19 cm
Shoulder to sole of foot	6 inches	15 cm
Shoulder to waist	1¾ inches	4.5 cm
Underarm to waist	¾ inch	2 cm
Arm (underarm to wrist)	1¼ inches	3 cm
Width around at underarm	4¼ inches	11 cm
Width around at waist	4 inches	10 cm
Waist to crotch	1½ inches	4 cm
Waist to ankle	3¾ inches	9.5 cm
Inside leg (crotch to ankle)	2½ inches	6.5 cm
Width around head	5 inches	13 cm

Kestner 155: 1900-1925 model

Height	7 inches	18 cm
Shoulder to sole of foot	5½ inches	14 cm
Shoulder to waist	1½ inches	4 cm
Underarm to waist	½ inch	1.5 cm
Arm (underarm to wrist)	1¼ inches	3 cm
Width around at underarm	4 inches	10 cm
Width around at waist	4 inches	10 cm
Waist to crotch	1½ inches	4 cm
Waist to ankle	3½ inches	9 cm
Inside leg (crotch to ankle)	1¾ inches	4.5 cm
Width around head	4½ inches	11.5 cm

Simon & Halbig/ S&H/1078: 1900-1925 model

Height	8 inches	20 cm
Shoulder to sole of foot	6 inches	15 cm
Shoulder to waist	2 inches	5 cm
Underarm to waist	1 inch	2.5 cm
Arm (underarm to wrist)	1¾ inches	4.5 cm
Width around at underarm	4¾ inches	12 cm
Width around at waist	4½ inches	11.5 cm
Waist to crotch	1½ inches	4 cm
Waist to ankle	4 inches	10 cm
Inside leg (crotch to ankle)	2½ inches	6.5 cm
Width around head	5 inches	13 cm

Chapter 1

UNDIES: Panties, Undershirts & Half-slips

In this chapter, instructions are given on how to make undergarments in both knitting and crochet, using different yarns and needles, etc. for several sizes of dolls. It is very important to list panties by waist size, as dolls of varying heights are often able to wear the same panties, depending on their waist size. For example, the 6-inch Hitty by Raikes Collectibles and the 8-inch Betsy McCall by the Tonner Doll Company can both wear the same size panties, and the 8-inch composition Patsy-type and 7½-inch hard-plastic dolls of the 1950s can often wear the same size panties. Some of the dresses and skirts that are full look better with a half-slip underneath. To adjust the half-slip patterns, thread elastic through at the waistline to narrow the waist, and often the slip can be shortened or lengthened to suit the height of the doll.

*Knitted Panties

Abigail

3½-inch (9-cm) waist

This quick-to-knit pair of panties fits many of the dolls in the 6-inch (15 cm) to 9-inch (23 cm) range that have waists measuring from 3½ to 4 inches (9 to 10 cm). Version A is worn by an 8-inch Betsy McCall doll by the Tonner Doll Company; Version B is worn by an 8-inch doll by the Alexander Doll Company.

Both pairs of panties can be easily adjusted to fit different waists by threading thin elastic through the ribbing stitches at the waist. They can easily be lengthened or shortened by working more or less rows before or after decreasing

Version A is knitted in st. st with k1, p1 rib at the waist. Version B is knitted entirely in ms.st (seed st), except for the ribbing at waist.

Materials

Small amount of DMC Babylo 10 or equivalent

#0 US (2 mm) [14] knitting needles

Length of thin elastic, if needed

Measurements

Because one pair of panties is knitted in st.st and one in ms.st, there is a slight difference in the size of the finished garments

Version A

Length of waist to crotch	1 3/8 inches (3.5 cm)
Length of side seam	7/8 inch (1.5 cm)
Width around at waist	3½ inches (9 cm)

Version B

Length of waist to crotch	1½ inch (4 cm)
Length of side seam	7/8 inch (1.5 cm)
Width around at waist	3½ inches (9 cm)

Tension

12 sts = 1 inch (2.5 cm)

16 rows = 1 inch (2.5 cm)

Version A

Version B

Instructions

Version A

Cast on 20 st

Work 4 rows of k1, p1 rib

***Work 8 rows in st.st

Cast off 2 sts at beg of the next 8 rows (4 sts)

Work 4 rows of st.st on these 4 sts

Cast on 2 sts at beg of the next 8 rows (20 sts)

Work 8 rows of st.st***

Work 4 rows of k1, p1, rib

Cast off

Version B

Work first 4 rows as Version A, inc. 1 st at end of last row of rib (21 sts), then work rest of garment entirely in ms.st as per instructions from *** to ***, dec 1 st at end of row (20 sts), then k1, p1 rib section as at end of Version A

To Make Up

Sew up side seams. If you wish, sew lace around each leg opening. If the waist is too large for the doll, thread a length of thin elastic through the ribbing stitches at waist.

Aileen

4-inch (10-cm) waist

This easy-to-make pair of crocheted panties, with a contrast trim at the leg openings, is worn by a 2006 7½-inch Ginny by the Vogue Doll Company.

Materials

Small ball of No. 10 mercerized crochet cotton in main color (MC)
Small amount of No. 10 mercerized crochet cotton in contrasting color (CC)
#8 US (1.25 mm) crochet hook
Length of thin elastic, if needed

Measurements

Length from waist to crotch	1¾ inches (4.5 cm)
Length of side seam	1¼ inches (3 cm)
Width around at waist	4 inches (10 cm)

Tension

10 dc = 1 inch (2.5 cm)
6 rows of sc plus 5 rows of dc = 1 inch (2.5 cm)

Instructions

Make 22 ch, turn, miss 2 ch
1st row: 1 sc in each chain (20 sc), 3 ch, turn
2nd row: 1 dc in each st (20 dc) 2 ch, turn
Repeat last 2 rows 5 times
Next row: sl.st the first 7 sts, 1 sc in the next 8 sts, 3 ch, turn
2nd row: 8 dc, 2 ch, turn
3rd row: miss 1 dc, 6 sc, 3 ch, turn
4th row: miss 1 sc, 4 dc, 3ch turn
5th row: 4 dc, 2 ch, turn
6th row: inc in the 1st st, 2 sc, inc in the last st (6 sc), 3 ch, turn
7th row: inc in the 1st st, 4 dc, inc in the last st (8 dc), 9 ch, turn
8th row: miss the first 2 ch, 1 sc each of the next 7 ch, 8 sc, 10 ch, turn
9th row: miss the first 3 ch, 1 dc in each of the next 7 ch, 1 dc in each remaining dc (20 dc), 2 ch, turn
10th row: 20 sc, 3 ch, turn
11th row: 20 dc, 2 ch, turn.
Repeat last 2 rows 4 times
Repeat 10th row
Fasten off
Leg Opening Trim
Open out panties, so you can work easily around each leg opening. Starting at beginning of one leg opening, and using contrasting color, work *1 sc, then 3 dc shell evenly, all around leg opening. Work other leg opening to match.

To Make Up

Sew up side seam. If necessary, elastic may be threaded through first row of sc.

*Knitted Panties

Ailsa

5-inch (12.5-cm) waist

These panties can be quickly knitted for dolls with larger waists, such as a look-a-like composition Patsy.

Materials

Small amount of DMC Perle No. 5 or Pelican Perle No. 5, or equivalent

#0 US (2 mm) [14] knitting needles

Measurements

Length from waist to crotch	1¾ inches (4.5 cm)
Length of side seam	1¼ inches (3 cm)
Width around at waist (unstretched)	4½ inches (11.5 cm)

Tension

11 sts = 1 inch (2.5 cm)

16 rows = 1 inch (2.5 cm)

Instructions

Cast on 24 sts

Work 4 rows in k1, p1, rib

Work 4 rows of st.st

Inc 1 st at each end of the next row, and then in the following 4th row 2 times (30 st)

Dec, by knitting k2 tog at each end of the next 13 rows

Work 3 rows on the remaining 4 sts

Inc 1 st at each end of the next 12 rows (30 sts)

Dec 1 st at each end of the next row and in the following 4th row: row: 2 times (24 sts)

Work 4 rows of st.st

Work 4 rows in k1, p1, rib

To Make Up

Pick up and knit 24 sts evenly, around each leg opening. Work 3 rows of k1, p1 rib. Cast off in rib.

Alice

4-inch (10-cm) chest

Very versatile, this pattern can be made into a simple undershirt, as seen in Version A, or as a simple sleeveless blouse that can be worn under a jacket. When worked in a bright color, it makes a nice summer top, like the one worn by an 8-inch doll by the Alexander Doll Company in Version B.

Materials

1 ball of Perle No. 8 cotton (DMC or equivalent)
#0 US (2 mm) [14] knitting needles
2 #4/0 (000 or 5 mm) snaps or hooks & eyes or Velcro strip

Measurements

Shoulder to hem	2¾ inches (7 cm)
Shoulder to hem (hem turned up)	2 3/8 inches (6 cm)
Width around at underarm	4 inches (10 cm)
Width around at hem	5 inches (13 cm)

Tension

12 st = 1 inch (2.5 cm)
14 rows = 1 inch (2.5 cm)

Version A: Undershirt

Version B: Sleeveless Blouse

Instructions

Cast on 30 sts
1st row: knit
2nd row: purl
3rd row: knit
4th row: p1, *m1, p2 tog, repeat from * to last st, p1
Work 6 rows in st.st, starting with a knit row
K2 tog at each end of next row and every 6th row, until 24 sts remain
Purl 1 row
Armhole Shaping
Cast off 3 sts at beginning of next 2 rows
Work 4 rows in st.st
Neck Shaping: First Side
K4, cast off 10 st, k4
Work 5 rows of st.st on the last 4 sts
Cast off
Neck Shaping: Second Side
Rejoin yarn to other side of neck, and work 5 rows in st.st
Cast off
Work a second piece the same way
Neck Edging
Sew up one shoulder. Pick up and knit 48 sts evenly around neck.
1st row: p1, *m1, p2 tog, repeat from * to end of row
2nd row: cast off, using knit st
First Armhole Edging (one shoulder seam sewn)
Starting at one side edge, pick up and knit 26 sts evenly around armhole
Repeat 1st & 2nd row of neck edging
Cast off, using knit st
Second Armhole Edging (shoulder seam not sewn)
Starting at one shoulder, pick up and knit 26 sts evenly around armhole
Repeat 1st & 2nd row of neck edging
Cast off, using knit st

To Make Up

Gently fold the neck edging over, so as to form a series of picot, and sew in place around neck. Repeat process for each armhole. Sew up side seams. You may also like to fold hem under along the line of m1, p2 tog, and carefully sew the hem formed on the inside of the garment, thus forming a picot-style hem as seen on Version B, the sleeveless blouse.

*Crocheted Half-Slip

Amanda

4-inch (10-cm) waist

This lovely little half-slip, in woolen yarn, can be worn under many of the fuller-skirted dresses. When worked in a thinner yarn, such as DMC Babylo 10, it is suitable for other dresses, as well. If necessary, thread elastic through at the waistline to narrow the waist, and often the slip can be shortened or lengthened to suit the height of the doll

Materials: Version A	**Version B**
½ ounce (25 gm) white 2 ply yarn or equivalent	½ ball DMC Babylo 10
#1 US (2 mm) crochet hook	#8 US (1.25 mm) crochet hook
Short length of thin elastic, if needed	10 inches (25 cm) thin ribbon

Measurements	**Version A**	**Version B**
Length from waist to hem	2¼ inches (5.5 cm)	2 inches (5 cm)
Width around waist	4½ inches (11.5 cm)	4 inches (10 cm)
Width around hem	6½ inches (16.5 cm)	6 inches (15 cm)

Tension: Version A	**Version B**
7 dc = 1 inch (2.5cm)	8 dc = 1 inch (2.5cm)
2 rows = ½ inch (1.25cm)	2 rows = ½ inch (1.25cm)

Version A: Woolen Yarn

Instructions (work both versions the same way)

Using white yarn, work 34 ch

1st row: work 1 dc into 4th ch for hook, then work 1 dc in each ch to end, 3 ch, turn

2nd row: work 1 dc into each space (between each of the dc) in the previous row, 1 dc on last dc, 2 ch, turn

3rd row: 1 sc in each dc, 2 ch, turn

4th row: *4 sc, 2 sc into next sc, repeat from * to end of row, 3 ch, turn

5th row: 1 dc into each sc, 3ch, turn

6th row: work as 2nd row

7th row: work as 2nd row

8th row: 1 sc into 1st dc, *3 ch, miss 1 dc, 1 sc into next dc, repeat to end of row, 4 ch, turn

9th row: *1 sc into 3 ch loop, 3 ch, repeat from * to end of row, finishing with 1 ch, 1 dc into loop

10th row: work as 9th row, join to beginning of row

11th round: sl st into 1st 3 ch loop *work 3 ch, 2 dc, sl st into next 3 ch loop, repeat from * to end of row

12th round: sl st into 3 ch loop, *work 3 ch, 2 dc, sl st into next 3 ch loop, repeat from * to end of row

Fasten off

To Make Up

Sew up back seam from the 10th to the 5th row. Thread ribbon through 1st row of dc to fit waist.

Version B: DMC Babylo 10

Amy

3½- to 4-inch (9- to 10-cm) waist

This knitted half-slip is ideal for wearing under many of the dresses featured in Chapter 2.

Materials

Small amount of DMC Babylo 10 or equivalent
#0 US (2 mm) [14] knitting needles
Short length of thin elastic, if needed

Measurements

Waist to hem	2¼ inches (6 cm)
Width around at waist	4 inches (10 cm)
Width around at hem	9½ inches (24 cm)

Tension

12 sts = 1 inch (2.5 cm)
14 rows = 1 inch (2.5 cm)

Instructions

Back

Cast on 85 sts

1st row: purl

2nd row: k1 *m1, k1, sl. 1, k2 tog, psso, k1, m1, k1, repeat from * to end

3rd row: purl

Repeat last 2 rows 1 time

6th row: k1, then (k2 tog) 42 times (43 sts)

Beginning with a purl row, work 7 rows in st. st

14th row: Dec. 1 st at beginning and end of row

Repeat last 8 rows 1 time

Work 5 rows in st. st starting with a purl row

Next row: k1, *k2 tog, k1 rep from * to end

Purl 1 row

Next row: *k1, p1, repeat from * to last st, k1

Next row: *p1, k1, repeat from * to last st, p1

Repeat last 2 rows 1 time

Cast off

Front: Make the front the same way as the back.

To Make Up

Sew up side seams and, if necessary, thread thin elastic through the rib sts at waist, to fit the doll's waist.

Chapter 2

Dresses

In this chapter you will find a great variety of dresses, something to suit any doll in the small-size range, from simple to complicated, with long or short sleeves, and even sleeveless. Knitting patterns are offered for some of the dresses and crocheting patterns are offered for others, using a variety of yarns from fine crochet cotton to knitting cotton, as well as a wide range of needle and crochet-hook sizes. Whether you want something to make in an evening, or a more challenging long-term project, you will find it in this chapter.

Many of the dresses will fit dolls of other sizes than those given, depending on their waist and chest measurements. The dresses can easily be altered, either by adding a sash to bring in the waist, or by working rows of crochet down both sides of the back opening. By working less or more rows (or patterns), you can lengthen or shorten the bodices or the skirts to suit the height of a doll. For example, the same dress that fits Betsy McCall by the Tonner Doll Company and Riley by Kish & Company can, with a little extra added to the back opening, fit the chubbier 8-inch dolls by the Alexander Doll Company. A dress that fits a Raikes Collectibles' 6½-inch Hitty will also fit the English Amanda Jane doll, or an antique bisque-headed doll, or even a vintage hard-plastic Miss Curity, as well as other dolls in this small-size range. Remember that you can also adjust many of the dresses to fit dolls of different sizes by changing the size of your needles or hooks, or by using different yarns.

***Crocheted Dress with White Yoke

Beatrice

8 to 9 inches (20 to 23 cm) high

Lightly Lily, a 9-inch limited-edition doll by the Lawton Doll Company, wears a frock that matches her large navy bow (Version A). A smaller example of the frock is worn by an 8-inch antique Simon & Halbig 1078 doll with a bisque head and five-piece composition body (Version B).

Version A:
9-inch doll

Materials: Version A

1 ball of DMC Perle No. 5 or the equivalent, such as Pelicano Perle No. 5, in navy (MC)
1 ball 3 ply crochet silk, or equivalent, in white (CC)
#7 US (1.5 mm) crochet hook
3 #4/0 (000 or 5 mm) snaps

Materials: Version B

1 ball DMC Babylo 10 or equivalent in main color (MC)
Small amount DMC Babylo 10 in white or contrasting color (CC)
#8 US (1.25 mm) crochet hook
2 #4/0 (000 or 5 mm) snaps

Measurements	**Version A**	**Version B**
Length from shoulder to hem	5 inches (12.5 cm)	4 inches (10 cm)
Length from dropped waist to hem	2½ inches (6.5 cm)	1¾ inches (4.5 cm)
Width around at underarm	4¼ inches (11 cm)	3½ inches (9 cm)
Width around at hem	11 inches (28 cm)	8 inches (20 cm)
Length of sleeve seam	2 inches (5 cm)	1 5/8 inches (4 cm)

Tension: Version A

8 dc = 1 inch (2.5 cm)
3 rows of sc plus 3 rows of dc = 1 inch (2.5 cm)

Tension: Version B

10 dc = 1 inch (2.5 cm)
4 rows of sc plus 3 rows dc = 1 inch (2.5 cm)

Instructions

Skirt (worked from the base of yoke to hem)

Using MC, make 33 ch, miss 2 ch, turn

1st row: working into the top portion of each ch only, work 1sc in each ch, (31 sc) 3 ch, turn

2nd row: 1 dc in each st, 2 ch, turn

3rd row: 1 sc in each st, 3 ch, turn

Repeat the last 2 rows 3 times

10th row: *1 dc in first st, 2 dc in next st, repeat from * to last st, 1 dc, 2 ch, turn

11th row: 1 sc in each st, 3 ch, turn

12th row: *1 dc in each first 2 st, 2 dc in next st, repeat from * to last st, 1 dc (61 st) 2ch, turn

13th row: 1 sc in each st, 3 ch, turn

14th row: *1 dc in each first 3 sts, 2 dc in next, repeat from * to last st, 1 dc (76 sts), 2 ch, turn

15th row: 1 sc in each st, 3 ch, turn

16th row: 1 dc in each st, 2 ch, turn

Repeat last 3 rows 2 times

Fasten off

Bodice

Back: First Side (working from yoke to the shoulder)

Using CC, with right side of work facing towards you, start at the back edge and work 1 sc into the top loop of the first 8 of the original ch sts, 2 ch, turn

2nd row: 1 sc in each st to end, 2 ch, turn (8 sc)

Repeat the last row 5 times

8th row: 1 sc in each of the first 4 sts, 2 ch, turn

9th row: 1 sc in each st, 2 ch, turn

Repeat the last row

Fasten off

Top Front

Miss 1 st of the original chain

1st row: work 1 sc in each of the next 13 sts, 2 ch, turn

2nd row: 1 sc in each st, 2 ch, turn

Repeat last row 4 times

Neck Shaping: First Side

7th row: 1 sc in each of first 3 sts, miss 1 st, 1 sc in next st, 2 ch, turn

8th row: 4 sc, 2 ch, turn

9th row: 4 sc

Fasten off

Neck Shaping: Second Side

1st row: miss 3 st., rejoin yarn and work 1 sc in each sts to end, 2 ch, turn

2nd row: 1 sc in first 4 sts, 2 ch, turn

3rd row: 4 sc, 2 ch, turn

4th row: repeat 3rd row

Fasten off

Back: Second Side

Miss 1 st of original chain sts, using CC

1st row: work 1 sc in each of the remaining 8 sts, 2 ch, turn

2nd row: 1 sc in each of the 8 sc, 2 ch, turn

Repeat the last row 5 times

8th row: sl.st 4 sts, 1 sc in each st to end, 2 ch, turn

9th row: 1 sc in each 4 sts

Repeat 9th row

Fasten off

Yoke Trim

Sew up both shoulder seams. With wrong side of work towards you, and starting at the back edge, fold yoke over where it joins to the top of the bodice.

Work 1 sc into first space between the folded-over sts, *2 ch, 1 sc in next space, repeat to end of back (1 sc, 2 ch, three times

Version B: 8-inch doll

in corner st), then 1 sc, 2 ch, at each end of sc rows around shoulder opening (1 sc, 2 ch, three times in the corner st) 1 sc, 2 ch, in each space of fold over, across front, (1 sc, 2 ch, 3 times in the corner st) 1 sc, 2ch at end of each sc row around shoulder opening, (1sc, 2 ch, three times in the corner st) 1 sc, 2 ch in each space between sts of yoke fold over, finishing with a sc in last space.

Next row: 4 ch * 1 sc in 2 ch space, 2 ch, repeat from * working 1 sc, 2 ch, 3 times into each of the corner sts

Next row: 3 ch, 1 dc into first 2 ch space, * 3 dc in next 2 ch space, 1 sc in next, repeat from * to end

Fasten off

Neck Edging

Using CC, with right side of work facing you, work 26 sc evenly around neck

Next row: working into the back of the top loop only of each of the previous 26 sc, work as follows, *1 sc, 3 ch, miss 1 sc, repeat from * to end, finishing with 1 sc

Next row: fold previous row down on yoke, work 1 sc in the other top loop of each of the original row of 26 sc of neck trim.

Fasten off

Note: for a chubbier doll, work 2 rows of sc or 1 row of dc down each side of back opening.

Sleeves (make 2)

Cuff

Using CC, beginning at the cuff edge, work 16 ch, miss 3 ch, turn

1st row: work 1 dc in each ch (13 dc), 2 ch, turn

2nd row: working into the front loop only of each st in previous row, work as follows, *1 sc, 3 ch, miss 1 st, repeat to last st, 1 sc, 2 ch, turn

3rd row: *1 sc in ch sp, 3 ch, repeat from * to end, finishing with a dc in last st

Fasten off

Sleeve

Join in MC, working in the back loop only of each st, in the 1st row at beginning of cuff, work 2 dc in 1st st, then 1 dc in each st, to
last st, 2 dc in last st (15 dc) 2 ch, turn

2nd row: 1 sc in each st, 3 ch, turn

3rd row: 1 dc in each st, 2 ch, turn

4th row: 2 sc in first st, 1 sc in each st, to last st, 2 sc in last st, 3 ch, turn

5th row: repeat 3rd row (17 dc)

6th row: repeat 4th row (19 dc)

7th row: repeat 3rd row

8th row: 1 sc in each st, 3 ch, turn

9th row: 1 dc in each st, 2 ch, turn

*Repeat the last two rows 1 time and the 8th row again * (or to length desired)

Version B: omit from * to * of the last instruction

Sleeve Top Shaping

13th row: miss 1 st, 1 dc in each st, to last 2 sts, miss 1 st, 1 dc in last st, 2 ch, turn (17 dc)

14th row: miss 1 st, 1 sc in each st to last 2 st, miss 1 st, 1 sc in last st, 3 ch, turn (15 sc)

15th row: repeat 13th row (13 dc)

16th row: repeat 14th row (11 sc)

Fasten off

To Make Up

Sew sleeves in place, making sure you don't catch in the frill around the yoke. Sew up sleeve seams, leaving cuff seams to be sewn with contrast thread. Sew up back seam from hem for 2½ inches. Sew snaps to close back opening.

Bea

7½ to 9 inches (19 to 23 cm) high

This lovely lacy frock is suitable for a range of dolls; Version A is suitable for any with a 5-inch (12.5-cm) waist, including 8- to 9-inch models such as the composition look-a-like Patsy. The smaller Version B fits a 7½-inch Riley by Kish & Company as well as others of this height, such as an antique 7½-inch K*R Halbig doll.

Materials: Version A

2 balls No. 8 mercer perle crochet cotton (the cheaper version is softer in texture than the more expensive DMC or Coats No. 8) or equivalent

#1 US (2.25 mm) [13] knitting needles

3 #4/0 (000 or 5 mm) snaps

1 yard (meter) of matching narrow ribbon

Materials: Version B

1 spool Cameo yarn (used for punch embroidery) or equivalent, such as fine 2 ply yarn

#0 US (2 mm) [14] knitting needles

2 #4/0 (000 or 5 mm) snaps

1 yard (meter) of matching narrow ribbon

Measurements	**Version A**	**Version B**
Length from shoulder to hem	4¼ inches (11 cm)	3¾ inches (9.5 cm)
Width around at underarm	5 inches (12.5 cm)	3½ inches (9 cm)
Width around at hem	10 inches (25 cm)	7 inches (18 cm)
Length of sleeve seam	¾ inches (2 cm)	½ inch (1.5 cm)

Tension: Version A	**Version B**
10 sts = 1 inch (2.5 cm)	12 sts = 1 inch (2.5 cm)
6 patterns = 1 inch (2.5 cm)	7 patterns = 1 inch (2.5 cm)

Version B: 7½-inch doll

Instructions

Skirt

Starting at the hem, cast on 100 sts, and knit 3 rows in garter st

Pattern

1st row: k1, *k2, sl 1, k2 tog, psso, k2, m1, repeat from * to last st, k1

2nd row: k1, *p6, m1, repeat from * to last st, k1

Repeat last 2 rows 12 times

Dec row: *k2 tog, repeat all along row (50 sts)

1st row: knit

2nd row: k2 *m1, k2 tog, k1, repeat to end of row.

3rd row: knit 1 row

4th row: knit

5th row: purl

Repeat last 2 rows 2 times

Divide for armholes: k12, cast off 2, k21, cast off 2, k11

Bodice

Back: First Side

On the last 12 sts, knit 10 rows in st.st (9 rows on second half back)

Cast off 6 sts

Knit 1 row

Purl 1 row

Next row: k4, k2 tog

Cast (bind) off remaining sts

Top Front

Rejoin yarn next to the 2 cast-off sts, and on the next 22 sts

Work 6 rows in st.st

1st row: knit

2nd row: k1, m1, k2 tog, k1, repeat from * to end of row

3rd row: knit

4th row: knit

5th row: knit

6th row: purl

Neck Shaping: First Side

Next row: k8, cast off 6 sts, k8, turn

On the last 7 sts: p6, p2 tog

2nd row: k2 tog, k5

3rd row: purl

4th row: knit

Cast off

Rejoin yarn to other side of neck

Neck Shaping: Second Side

Next row: p2 tog, purl to end of row

2nd row: k5, k2 tog

3rd row: purl

4th row: knit

Cast off

Back: Second Side

Rejoin yarn to remaining sts

Work 9 rows in st.st

Cast off 6 sts at beginning of row

2nd row: purl

3rd row: knit

4th row: p4, p2 tog

Cast off

Sleeves (make 2)

Cast on 16 sts, and work 3 rows in garter st

Next row: *k1, inc in the next, repeat from * to end of row (24 sts)

Work 5 rows in st.st

Sleeve Top Shaping

Continue in st.st, decreasing 1 st at both ends of needle in each row, until 10 sts remain

Cast off

To Make Up

Sew up shoulder seams. Sew sleeves in place. Sew up back seam to within ½-inch of waist. Thread thin ribbon through waist. Thread matching ribbon through area on yoke, and finish with a bow.

Optional Neck Edging

If you wish, pick up 34 sts evenly around neck

1st row: *k1, inc by knitting in front, then back, then front again of next st, repeat from * to end of row

2nd row: cast off all stitches

Version B:
7½-inch doll

Version A:
9-inch doll

Becky

8 to 9 inches (20 to 23 cm) high

A 9-inch doll by German artist Heidi Plusczok and a 1960s English Patch (similar to Ideal's Pepper, made in the same era), also 9 inches high (both Version A), wear variations on this pretty party dress with a bertha collar. The 8-inch Alexander Doll Company model wears the same pattern with a contrasting collar, which has been knit entirely in DMC Babylo 10 with smaller needles (Version B).

Materials: Version A

1 ball of DMC Babylo 10 or equivalent
#2 US (2.75 mm) [12] knitting needles
#1 US (2.25 mm) [13] knitting needles
3 #4/0 (000 or 5 mm) snaps or Velcro strips

Materials: Version B

1 ball of DMC Babylo 10 or equivalent in main color (MC)
Small amount of DMC Babylo 10 or equivalent, in contrasting color (CC) for collar
#0 US (2 mm) [14] knitting needles
2 #4/0 (000 or 5 mm) snaps

Measurements	Version A	Version B
Length from shoulder to hem	4½ inches (11.5 cm)	4 inches (10 cm)
Length from waist to hem	2¾ inches (7 cm)	2½ inches (6.5 cm)
Width around at chest	4½ inches (11.5cm)	3¾ inches (9.5 cm)
Width around at hem	9 inches (23 cm)	8 inches (20 cm)
Length of collar: neck to hem	1 inch (1.25 cm)	1 inch (1.25 cm)

Tension: Version A	Version B
1 pattern across = 1 inch (2.5 cm)	1 pattern across = 7/8 inch (2 cm)
10 sts across st. st = 1 inch (2.5 cm)	11 sts = 1 inch (2.5 cm)
4 patterns = 1 inch (2.5 cm)	4 patterns = ¾ inch (2 cm)

Version A: 9-inch doll

Instructions

Skirt

Version A: Using #2 US (2.75 mm) [12] needles, cast on 90 st
Version B: Using #0 US (2 mm) [14] needles
Starting at the hem, work 3 rows in garter st
Work in pattern as follows:
1st row: k1, (k2 tog) twice, *(m1, k1) three times, m1, (k2 tog) 4 times, repeat from * until 8 sts remain, (m1, k1) 3 times, m1, (k2 tog) twice, k1
2nd row: purl
3rd row: knit
4th row: purl
Repeat last 4 rows of pattern 7 times
Dec row: k2 tog all along row (45 sts)

Bodice

Version A: Change to #1 US (2.25 mm) [13] needles
Version B: Do not change needles
Starting with a purl row, work 9 rows in st. st
Divide for armholes: k10, cast off 3, k18, cast off 2, k9
Back: First Side
Work 10 rows in st. st
1st row: cast off 5 sts, purl to end
2nd row: knit
3rd row: p2 tog, purl to end
4th row: knit
5th row: purl
Cast off remaining sts
Top Front
Rejoin yarn to wrong side of center 19 sts, and work 7 rows in st.st, starting with a purl row
Neck Shaping: First Side
K7, cast off 5 sts, k7
1st row: purl
2nd row: k2 tog, knit to end
3rd row: purl
Repeat last 2 rows 1 time
Cast off remaining sts
Neck Shaping: Second Side
Rejoin yarn to other side of neck
1st row: purl
2nd row: knit to last 2 sts, k2 tog
3rd row: purl
Repeat last 2 rows 1 time
Cast off remaining sts
Back: Second Side
Rejoin yarn on wrong side of remaining sts, starting with a purl row, work 9 rows in st.st
Neck Shaping
Cast off 5 sts, knit to end
Purl 1 row
Next row: k2 tog, knit to end of row
Purl 1 row
Cast off

Collar

Version A: Using #1 US (2.25 mm) [13] needles
Version B: Do not change needles
Cast on 68 sts
Work 3 rows in garter st
1st row: k1, (k2 tog) twice, * (m1, k1) 3 times; m1, (k2 tog) 4 times; repeat from * to last 8 sts., (m1, k1) 3 times; m1, (k2 tog) twice, k1
2nd row: purl
Repeat last 2 rows 5 times
Cast off loosely

To Make Up

Sew up shoulder seams. (If you wish, you may pick up and knit the stitches around each armhole, then cast off using a purl st) Fold the collar in half and mark with a pin. Place a pin at center of front neck. Matching center pin, place the collar, from the back neck shaping on one side to the other, and sew into position. Sew on snaps or Velcro strips to close the back opening.

Version B: 8-inch doll

Version A: 9-inch doll

Belinda

7 to 9 inches (18 to 23 cm) high

These crocheted dresses with striped skirts are worn by four models: 9-inch Lightly Lily by The Lawton Doll Company and a 9-inch wooden doll by Raikes Collectibles wear the long-sleeved version, while German artist Heidi Plusczok's 9-inch doll and a 7-inch Amanda Jane wear the short-sleeved wide-collared variations.

Version A:
9-inch doll

Materials: Version A

1 ball of DMC Perle No. 5, or Pelicano No. 5 or equivalent in main color (MC)
1 ball DMC Petra No. 5 or equivalent in contrasting color (CC)
#7 US (1.5 mm) crochet hook
3 #4/0 (000 or 5 mm) snaps

Materials: Version 1B

½ ball of DMC Babylo 10 or equivalent in main color (MC)
½ ball of DMC Babylo 10 or equivalent in contrasting color (CC)
#8 US (1.25 mm) crochet hook
3 #4/0 (000 or 5 mm) snaps
Buttons for front decoration, if desired

Materials: Version 2B

1 ball DMC Perle No. 8 cotton or equivalent in main color (MC)
1 ball DMC Perle No. 8 cotton or equivalent in contrasting color (CC)
#8 US (1.25 mm) crochet hook
2 #4/0 (000 or 5 mm) snaps
Buttons for front decoration, if

Measurements		**Version 1B**	**Version 2B**
Length from shoulder to he		4½ inches (11.5 cm)	3¾ inches (9.5 cm)
Length from waist to hem		½ inches (6.5 cm)	2 inches (5 cm)
Width around at undera		(7 cm)	3 inches (7.5 cm)
Width around at hem			6½ inches (16.5 cm)
Length of sleeve sea			½ inch (1 cm)

Tension: Version
8 dc = 1 inch (2
3 rows of dc p
Tension: Ve
9 dc = 1 in
2 rows of
Tension
4 rows

Abb
H hook, draw through the same stitch, wrap yarn over the

Instructions

(use same instructions for all versions, except where noted)

Skirt (worked sideways)

Version A: use pink DMC Perle No. 5 (MC)
Version 1B: use green DMC Babylo 10 (MC)
Version 2B: use brown DMC Perle No. 8 (MC)
Make 23 ch, turn, miss 2 ch
1st row: 1 sc in each ch, (21 sc) 3 ch, turn
2nd row: 1 dc in each of the next 15 sc, 1 hdc in each of the next 3 sc, 1 sc in each of the last 3 sc, 2ch, turn, change to contrasting color (CC)
3rd row: 1 sc in each sc, 3 ch, turn
4th row: 15 dc, 3 hdc, 3 sc, change to MC, 2 ch, turn
5th row: 21 sc, 3 ch, turn
6th row: 15 dc, 3 hdc, 3 sc, change to CC, 2 ch, turn
Repeat last 4 rows 9 times, then 3rd & 4th row 1 time
Fasten off

Bodice

Using MC, work along the end of the rows on the short side of work, working 2 sc in the end of each CC sc row, 1 sc in end of each MC sc row (33 sc), 2 ch, turn

Version A:
9-inch doll

Version 2B:
7½-inch doll

1st row: 33 sc, 3 ch, turn
2nd row: 33 dc, 2 ch, turn
3rd row: 33 sc, 2 ch, turn
4th row: 33 sc, 3 ch, turn
5th row: 33 dc, 2 ch, turn
6th row: 33 sc, 2 ch, turn
Back: First Side
7th row: 8 sc, 3 ch, turn
8th row: 8 dc, 2 ch, turn
9th row: 8 sc, 2 ch, turn
10th row: 8 sc, 3 ch, turn
11th row: 8 dc, 2 ch, turn
12th row: 4 sc, 2 ch, turn
13th row: 4 sc
Fasten off
Top Front
Return to base of back, miss 1 st, join in yarn and work 1 sc in each of the next 15 sts, 3 ch, turn
2nd row: 15 dc, 2 ch, turn
3rd row: miss 1 sc, 12 sc, miss 1 sc, 1 sc in last st (13 sc) 2 ch, turn
4th row: 13 sc, 3 ch, turn
Neck Shaping: First Side
5th row: 5 dc, 2 ch, turn
6th row: miss 1 sc, 4 sc, 2 ch, turn
7th row: 4 sc, 3 ch, turn
8th row: 4 dc
Fasten off
Neck Shaping: Second Side
1st row: miss 3 sc, 5 dc, 2 ch, turn
2nd row: 3 sc, miss 1 st, 1 sc in last st, 2 ch, turn
3rd row: 4 sc, 3 ch, turn
4th row: 4 dc
Fasten off
Back: Second Side
Miss 1 st (for armhole), rejoin yarn and work 1 sc in remaining 8 sts, 3 ch, turn
2nd row: 8 dc, 2 ch, turn
3rd row: 8 sc, 2 ch, turn
4th row: 8 sc, 3 ch, turn
5th row: 8 dc
6th row: slip st 4 sts, 4 sc, 2 ch, turn
7th row: 4 sc
Fasten off

Note: for a chubbier doll, work 2 rows of sc or one row of dc down each side of back opening.

Long Sleeves (make 2)

Cuff

**Using MC, make 5 ch, turn, miss 2 ch

1st row: 3 sc, ch, turn

2nd row: 3 sc, change to CC, 2 ch, turn

3rd row: 3 sc, 2 ch, turn

4th row: 3 sc, change to MC, 2 ch, turn

Repeat last 4 rows 3 times

Fasten off**

Sleeve

**Using MC, work 16 sc along one long edge of cuff, 2 ch, turn

2nd row: 16 sc, 3 ch, turn

3rd row: 16 dc, 2 ch, turn

4th row: 2 sc in 1st st, 14 sc, 2 sc in last st (18 sc), 2 ch, turn

5th row: 18 sc, 3 ch, turn

6th row: 18 dc, 2 ch, turn

7th row: 2 sc in 1st st, 16 sc, 2 sc in last st (20 sc) 2 ch, turn

8th row: 20 sc, 3 ch, turn

9th row: 20 dc, 2 ch turn

10th row: 20 sc, 2 ch, turn

11th row: 20 sc, 3 ch, turn

12th row: 20 dc, 2 ch, turn

13th row: 20 sc, 2 ch, turn

Version 1B:
9-inch doll

14th row: 20 sc, 3 ch, turn

15th row: miss 1 sc, 17 dc, miss 1 sc, 1 dc in last st, 2 ch, turn

16th row: miss 1 dc, 15 sc, miss 1 dc, 1 sc in last st, 2 ch, turn

17th row: miss 1 sc, 13 sc, miss 1 sc, 1 sc in last sc, 3 ch, turn

18th row: miss 1 sc, 11 dc, miss 1 sc, 1 dc in last st, 2 ch, turn

19th row: miss 1 dc, 10 sc

Fasten off

Short Sleeves (make 2)

Cuff

Work as cuff for long sleeve from ** to **

Sleeve

**Using MC, work 20 sc along long edge, 2 ch, turn

2nd row: 1 sc in each sc, 2 ch, turn

3rd row: miss 1 sc, 17 dc, miss 1 sc, 1 dc in last st, 2 ch, turn

4th row: miss 1 dc, 15 sc, miss 1 dc, 1 sc in last st, 2 ch, turn

5th row: miss 1 sc, 13 sc, miss 1 sc, 1 sc in last st, 3 ch, turn

6th row: miss 1 sc, 11 dc, miss 1 sc, 1 dc in last st, 2 ch, turn

7th row: miss 1 dc, 10 sc

Fasten off

Collar

Version A: 1 piece

Sew up shoulder seams

Work 30 sc around neck (working 3 sc in each corner of neck)

2nd row: 30 sc, 2 ch, turn

3rd row: *1 sc in next 2 sc, 2 sc in next sc, repeat to end of row, 3 ch, turn

4th row: 1 dc in each sc

Fasten off

Versions 1B & 2B: 2 pieces

Sew up shoulder seams

Mark the middle of the neck

Work 21 sc from the middle of neck to 2 sts, short of back opening, 2 ch, turn

2nd row: 21 sc, 2 ch, turn

3rd row: 21 sc, 3 ch, turn

4th row: 1 dc in each sc

Fasten off

Repeat for other side of neck

To Make Up

Sew sleeves in position; sew up sleeve seams. Sew up back seam from hem to within ½-inch of waist. Sew on snaps to close back opening. Fold collar over to front.

**Knitted Snow Maiden Dress

Beryl

6½ to 8 inches (16 to 20 cm) high

Wearing a silk rayon frock trimmed with faux fur is an 8-inch Betsy McCall by the Tonner Doll Company and an 8-inch doll by the Alexander Doll Company. A slightly smaller version of the dress with angora trim is worn by a 6½-inch Hitty doll by Raikes Collectibles. This pattern can be also be used to create a First Communion dress; to do so work 4 rows of moss stitch at the beginning of the pattern, instead of the faux-fur trim, and add a lace trim at the neckline and cuffs.

Version A:
8-inch doll

Materials: Version A

1 ball 3 ply silk yarn or equivalent
Small amount of fancy yarn, known as "Feathers/Lashes," or equivalent
#0 US (2 mm) [14] knitting needles
#2 US (2.75 mm) [12] knitting needles
2 #4/0 (000 or 5 mm) snaps

Materials: Version B

1 ball DMC Babylo 10 or DMC Cebelia No 10 or equivalent in main color (MC)
Small amount of angora or mohair for trim or use a contrasting color (CC)
#0 US (2 mm) [14] knitting needles
2 #4/0 (000 or 5 mm) snaps

Measurements	**Version A**	**Version B**
Shoulder to hem (minus trim)	4 inches (10 cm)	3½ inches (9 cm)
Width around at underarm	3½ inches (9 cm)	3½ inches (9 cm)
Width around at hem (minus trim)	11 inches (28 cm)	11 inches (28 cm)
Length of sleeve seam (minus trim)	2 inches (5 cm)	1¾ inches (4.5 cm)

Tension: Version A	**Version B**
12 sts = 1 inch (2.5 cm)	12 sts = 1 inch (2.5 cm)
13 rows = 1 inch (2.5 cm)	14 rows = 1 inch (2.5 cm)

Instructions

Skirt

Version A: Beginning at the hem, using "Feathers/Lashes" and #2 US (2.75 mm) [12] needles, cast on 105 sts. Break off yarn. Using #0 US (2mm) [14] needles join in 3 ply silk yarn.
Version B: Beginning at the hem and using mohair or angora yarn and #0 US (2 mm) [14] needles cast on 105 sts, break off yarn. Join in DMC Babylo 10 or equivalent and continue to use these needles throughout.
1st row: knit
2nd row: purl
3rd row: k2 tog, knit to last 2 sts, k2 tog (103 sts)
Beginning with a purl row, work 5 rows in st.st
9th row: k2 tog, (k9, k2 tog) 9 times
Purl 1 row, knit 1 row, purl 1 row
13th row: k2 tog, (k8, k2 tog) 9 times

Purl 1 row, knit 1 row, purl 1 row
17th row: (k2 tog, k7) 9 times
Purl 1 row, knit 1 row, purl 1 row
21st row: (k2 tog, k6) 9 times
Purl 1 row, knit 1 row, purl 1 row
25th row: (k2 tog, k5) 9 times
Purl 1 row, knit 1 row, purl 1 row
29th row: (k2 tog, k4) 9 times
30th row: purl
31st row: cast on 3 sts beg and end of row
32nd row: k3, purl to last 3 sts, k3
33rd row: waist decrease row, k3, *(k2 tog, k3), repeat from * to last 3 sts, k3 (40 sts)

Bodice

34th row: k3, purl to last 3 sts, k3
35th row: knit
Repeat 34th & 35th rows 2 times, then 34th row 1 time
Armhole row: k10, cast off 1 st, k17, cast off 1 st, k9
Back: First Side
Keeping the garter st border, and starting with a purl row, work 8 rows in st.st
Neck Shaping: Back
Cast off 5 sts, purl to end of row
Knit 1 row
Next row: p2 tog, purl to end
Cast off remaining sts
Top Front
Rejoin yarn to wrong side of 18 sts, and beginning with a purl row, work 5 rows in st.st
Neck Shaping: First Side
1st row: k6, cast off 6 sts, k6
2nd row: purl
3rd row: k2 tog, knit to end
4th row: purl
5th row: k2 tog, knit to end of row
Cast off remaining sts
Neck Shaping: Second Side
Rejoin yarn and purl 1 row
2nd row: knit to last 2 sts, k2 tog
3rd row: purl
4th row: knit to last 2 sts, k2 tog
Cast off remaining sts
Back: Second Side
Rejoin yarn, and beginning with a purl row, work 7 rows in st.st

Neck Shaping
Cast off 5 sts, knit to end of row
Purl 1 row
Next row: k2 tog, knit to end of row
Cast off remaining sts

Sleeves (make 2)

Version A: Using #2 US (2.75 mm) [12] needles and fancy yarn ("Feathers/Lashes"), cast on 13 sts. Break off yarn.
Using #0 US (2 mm) [14] needles and MC: knit one row
Version B: Using angora or mohair yarn and #0 US (2 mm) [14] needles: cast on 13 sts, end off yarn, join in MC and knit 1 row

Version B: 6½-inch doll

2nd row: purl
Versions A & B
3rd row: inc in 1st st, k5, inc, k5, inc in last st (16 sts)
Purl 1 row, knit 1 row, purl 1 row
7th row: knit, increasing in the 1st and last sts (18 sts)
Purl 1 row, knit 1 row, purl 1 row
11th row: work as 7th row (20 sts)
Work 5 rows in st.st
17th row: work as 7th row (22 sts)
Work 5 rows in st.st
Sleeve Top Shaping
Cast off 2 sts at beg of next 2 rows

Version A:
8-inch doll

Dec 1 st at each end of next 6 rows
Cast off remaining sts

Collar

Version A
Sew up shoulder seams. With right side of work facing you, and leaving the 2 st garter border free at both back edges, use silk yarn to pick up and knit 30 sts evenly around neck. Break off silk yarn, join in "Feathers/Lashes" or equivalent and work 1 row. Cast off.

Version B
Sew up shoulder seams. With right side of work facing you, and leaving the 2 st garter st border free at both back edges, use either mohair or angora yarn to pick up and knit 25 sts evenly around neck. Cast off.

To Make Up

Sew in sleeves, and sew up sleeve seams (wrapping the sleeve around a pencil makes it much easier to sew). Sew up back seam for 1¾ inches. Sew on two snaps to close back opening. If you wish, you may sew 3 small pearl buttons or beads down center front.

Note: for a thinner doll, like Betsy McCall, fold back opening ¼-inch on each side and carefully hem each side in position. Finish as larger version.

Beth

7½ to 8 inches (19 to 20 cm) high

Ready for stage in their tu-tus are 7½-inch Riley by Helen Kish and 8-inch Mary Englebreit's Ann Estelle by the Tonner Doll Company. (Directions for the beaded headband can be found on page 112.)

Version A: 7½-inch doll

Materials: Version A

2 balls of white DMC or Coats No. 20 crochet cotton if making the whole dress in white **or** 1 ball of white DMC or Coats No. 20 crochet cotton for bodice and top skirt
1 ball of light pink DMC or Coats No. 20 crochet cotton for second skirt
1 ball of darker pink DMC or Coats No. 20 crochet cotton for bottom skirt
#8 US (1.25 mm) crochet hook
3 #4/0 (000 or 5 mm) snaps or Velcro strips
Thin satin ribbon for shoulder straps, if you prefer

Materials: Version B

1 ball DMC or Coats No. 20 cotton in green for bodice
1 ball DMC or Coats No. 20 cotton in mauve for top skirt
1 ball DMC or Coats No. 20 cotton in lavender for second skirt
1 ball DMC or Coats No. 20 cotton in white for bottom skirt
Small amount of yellow DMC or Coats No. 20 cotton for trim on bottom skirt
#8 US (1.25 mm) crochet hook
3 #4/0 (000 or 5 mm) snaps
Beads or other decorative accents for bodice

Measurements	**Version A**	**Version B**
Length from top of bodice to waist	1 3/8 inches (3.5 cm)	1 3/8 inches (3.5 cm)
Length from shoulder to waist	2 inches (5 cm)	2 inches (5 cm)
Length from waist to hem top layer of skirt	1¼ inches (3 cm)	1½ inches (4 cm)
Width around at underarm	4 inches (10 cm)	4 inches (10 cm)
Width around at waist	4 inches (10 cm)	4 inches (10 cm)
Width around hem of top layer of skirt	30 inches (76 cm)	30 inches (76 cm)

Tension: Versions A & B

12 dc = 1 inch (2.5 cm)
5 rows of dc = 1 inch (2.5 cm)

Abbreviation Note

V: this stitch is used on all three of the skirts. It always consists of 1 dc, 1 ch, 1 dc, but can be made into either the 1 ch space made in the previous row or into the small space between two V's in the previous row.

Instructions

Bottom Skirt

Make 42 ch, turn

1st row: miss 2 ch, 1 sc in each of the ch to the end of the row (40 sc), 2 ch, turn

2nd row: 1 sc in each sc, 3 ch, turn

3rd row: 1 dc in first sc * 1 V in next sc, repeat to end of row, 1 dc in 3 ch of turning 3 ch, 3 ch, turn

4th row: *1 V into 1 ch space between the dc's in previous row, repeat to end of the row, work 1 dc in top ch of 3 turning ch in previous row, 3 ch, turn

5th row: *1 V into 1st ch space of previous row, into next ch space work 2 Vs (note: there is no ch st between the 2 V's), repeat to end of row, 1 dc in top of 3 turning ch, 3 ch, turn

6th row: 1 V into 1st 1 ch space, *1 V in next ch space, 1 V into space between the 2 V's, 1 V into next V, 1 V into next 1 ch space, repeat from * to end of row, 1 dc in 3rd ch of turning 3 ch, 3 ch, turn

Note: as Version B represents a flower, the 7th row of the bottom skirt can be worked in yellow, to represent pollen.

7th row: 1 V into 1st 1 ch space, *1 V into next ch space, 1 V into space between the 2 V's 1 V into next ch space, 1 V between the next 2 V's, 1 V into next 1 ch space, 1 V in next 1 ch space, repeat from * to end

Fasten off

Second Skirt

With white or designated color, work 1 sc into each of the original starting ch, 2 ch turn (40 sc)

Note: if you are unable to work into the original starting chain, work the second skirt separately, starting with 42 ch, 1st row turn, miss 2 ch, 1 sc in each chain to end (40 sc). Work second skirt as per above instructions, then carefully sew to the bottom skirt at waist.

Work 1 row of sc, into back loop only of each sc in previous row

Work 2nd to 6th rows as bottom skirt

7th row: 3 ch, then work 1 dc in every dc

Fasten off

Top Skirt

With wrong side of work facing you, work 1 sc into the front portion of each sc of second skirt (40 sc)

2nd row: 1 dc in front loop of each sc

Work 2nd to 7th rows as second skirt

Note: if you are unable to work the top skirt as one, with the two previous underskirts, make the top skirt separately, and carefully sew to the other two skirts at waist.

Bodice

With right side of work facing you, fold the top of the skirt over the lower tiers, and work 1 sc in each of the holes that are thus formed in the sc of top skirt. (It does take patience and a sharp hook, but it works.) (40 sc) 2 ch, turn

2nd row: 1 sc into each sc, 3 ch, turn

3rd row: 1 dc in each sc, 2 ch, turn

4th row: 1 sc in each dc, 2 ch, turn

5th row: 1 sc in each sc, 3 ch, turn

6th row: 1 dc in each sc, 2 ch, turn

Repeat last 3 rows 1 time

Fasten off

Top Front

1st row: miss the first 13 dc in from the back edge, join in yarn and work 1 sc in each of the next 14 dc, 2 ch, turn

2nd row: 1 sc in each of the 14 sc, 3 ch, turn

3rd row: 1 dc in each sc

Fasten off

Note: for dolls with a 4- to 5-inch chest, work 2 rows of sc down each side of back opening.

Shoulder Straps

Version A

Sew thin ribbon straps, one to each side of front, and then to back of bodice to length desired.

Version B

Join in yarn to one end of front bodice, work 3 sc, 2 ch, turn

2nd row: 3 sc, 3 ch, turn

3rd row: 3 dc, 2 ch, turn

Repeat first 3 rows 1 time, then 1st and 2nd row 1 time

Fasten off

For other strap, repeat at other side of front bodice. Try on doll, and pin straps in place on front bodice. Sew in place.

To Make Up

Carefully match the back edges of each layer of skirt, and keeping each layer of skirt separate, sew the three layers of skirt as follows:

Bottom skirt: Beginning at the hem, sew up the back edges of skirt together for 1 inch.

Second Skirt: Sew up back seam just as on the bottom skirt.

Top Skirt: Sew up back seam just as on the bottom skirt.

Sew snaps or Velcro strips to close back opening.

Version B:
8-inch doll

Betsy

8 inches (20 cm) high

The Vogue Doll Company's 2006 7½-inch Ginny models a summer version of this "smocked" frock, while an 8-inch antique Simon & Halbig 1078 shows off the winter version.

Materials: Version A

1 ball #10 crochet cotton or equivalent in main color (MC) (the cheaper #10 cotton gives a softer look than the more expensive DMC or Coats)
Small amount of same thread in white, or contrasting color (CC)
#0 US (2 mm) [14] knitting needles
3 #4/0 (000 or 5 mm) snaps or Velcro strips

Materials: Version B

1 spool Cameo yarn in main color (MC)
Small amount Cameo yarn in contrasting color (CC)
#0 US (2 mm) [14] knitting needles
3 #4/0 (000 or 5 mm) snaps or Velcro strips

Measurements: Version A

Length from shoulder to hem	3¾ inches (9.5 cm)
Length from waist to hem	2¼ inches (5.5 cm)
Width around at underarm	4 inches (10 cm)
Width around at hem	12 inches (30 cm)
Length of short-sleeve seam	¾ inch (1.5 cm)

Measurements: Version B

Length from shoulder to hem	4¼ inches (11 cm)
Length from waist to hem	2¼ inches (5.5 cm)
Width around at underarm	3½ inches (9 cm)
Width around at hem	12 inches (30 cm)
Length of long-sleeve seam	1¾ inches (4.5 cm)

Tension: Version A	**Version B**
13 sts = 1 inch (2.5 cm)	11 sts = 1 inch (2.5 cm)
14 rows = 1 inch (2.5 cm)	14 sts - inch (2.5 cm)

Version A: 7½-inch doll, summer dress

Instructions

Dress (worked in one piece, from the hem to the armholes)
Using main color (MC), cast on 145 sts
(Note: the following 6 rows give a scalloped effect to the hem.)
1st row: *k1, p1, k1, p1, sl.1, p1, k1, p1, k1, sl.1, repeat from * to last 5 sts, k1, p1, k1, p1, k1
2nd row: k1, p1, k1, p1, k1, *sl.1, k1, p1, k1, p1, sl.1, p1, k1, p1, k1, repeat from * to end
Repeat last 2 rows 2 times
7th row: knit
8th row: purl
Repeat last 2 rows 3 times
15th row: *k1, p1, repeat to last st, k1 (moss st or seed st)
Version A: Repeat 15th row 2 times
18th row: purl
19th row: knit
20th row: purl
21st to 23rd rows: work as 15th to 17th rows
24th row: purl
25th row: cast on 3 sts, knit to end
26th row: cast on 3 sts, purl to last 3 sts, k3
Version B: repeat 15th row 3 times
Work 4 rows st.st
Work 4 rows of ms.st
Knit one row, cast on on 3 sts
K3, purl to end, cast on 3 sts
Work Versions A & B the same for 27th & 28th rows
27th row: knit
28th row: k3, purl to last 3 sts, k3
Version A: Repeat last 2 rows 2 times
Version B: Repeat last 2 rows 3 times
To create waist: dec row k3, (k2 tog 6 times) then (k2 tog, k3 tog) 12 times, k1, (k2 tog, k3 tog) 12 times, (k2 tog 6 times), k3

Bodice

Work the following pattern throughout on all pieces of bodice. It creates a "broken rib'" effect as the base on which the "smocking" stitches are worked.
1st row: (wrong side of work) k3 *p1, k2, repeat from * to last st, k1
2nd row: k4 *p2, k1, repeat from * to last 3 sts, k3
Repeat last 2 rows 4 times, and then 1st row 1 time

Armhole Shaping: following the above pattern, work 17 sts, cast off 3 sts, work 26 sts, cast off 3 sts, work 16 sts

Back: First Side
1st row: k3, (p1, k2) 4 times, p2 tog
Working on these 16 sts, work 5 more rows, keeping to pattern
Neck Shaping
Cast off 7 sts, keeping to pattern
Keeping to pattern, work 1 row
Cast off remaining sts
Top Front
Rejoin thread to next set of sts
1st row: p2 tog, work in pattern to last 2 sts, p2 tog
Keeping to pattern, work 5 rows
Neck Shaping: First Side
Keeping to pattern, work 9 sts, then cast off 7 sts, work remaining 8 stitches in pattern
***Work 1 row in pattern on the remaining 9 sts
Keeping to pattern, dec 1 st at neck edge
Keeping to pattern, work one row
Cast off ***
Neck Shaping: Second Side
Rejoin thread to beginning of cast-off stitches, and keeping to pattern work from *** to ***
Back: Second Side
Rejoin yarn to remaining sts
1st row: p2 tog, work in pattern to end of row
Keeping to pattern, work 6 rows
Neck Shaping
Cast off 7 sts, keeping to pattern, work to end
Keeping to pattern, work 1 row
Cast off remaining sts

Sleeves: Version A (make 2)

Using white (or CC) yarn, cast on 17 sts
Work 3 rows in moss st
Next row: inc 1 st in each st (34 sts)
Starting with a purl row, work 5 rows in st.st
Sleeve Top Shaping
Cast off 3 sts at beg of next 2 rows
Dec 1 st at each end of next 4 rows
Next row: k2 tog all along row
Cast off remaining sts

Sleeves: Version B (make 2)

Using white (or CC) yarn, cast on 15 sts
Work 4 rows in moss st
Change to MC

Beginning with a knit row and working in st.st, inc 1 st at each end of next row, and every following 8th row, until you have 21 sts, ending on a knit row

Purl 1 row

Knit 1 row

Purl 1 row

Sleeve Top Shaping

K2 tog at the beginning of next 12 rows

Cast off remaining sts

Collar (make 2)

With white (or CC) yarn, cast on 19 sts

Work 4 rows in moss st

Dec 1 st at each end of the next 2 rows

Cast off in rib

To Make Up

Sew up the shoulder seams. Sew sleeves in place.

"Smocking" the Front Bodice

Thread a needle with a length of the CC and, starting at one back edge, at the base of the bodice ribbing, bring needle up though one of the k1 stitches, then under the next k1 rib stitch, then over and under the first stitch you came through, then oversew both stitches. Catch together the next 2 k1 rib stitches in the same way, and continue working in this fashion all along the row. Then work another row of "smocking" stitch in the same way on the 4th row, but this time catch together alternate k1 rib stitches. Repeat these two rows of "smocking" all over the bodice of the dress.

Mark the center of the neck, and sew one collar from this center point to back neck, leaving the 3-stitch underlap free. Sew other collar from center point to match. Sew up back seam to underlap. Sew underlap in position. Sew on snaps to close back opening.

Version B: 8-inch doll, winter dress

**Knitted Flower Girl Dress

Bettina

7½ to 8 inches (19 to 20 cm) high

This fancy dress is equally charming in a long version, as worn by a 7½-inch Riley by Kish & Company, or in a short one, as worn by an 8-inch 2006 doll by the Alexander Doll Company.

Version A: 7½-inch doll, long dress

Materials: Versions A & B

1 ball DMC Babylo 10 or equivalent

#0 US (2 mm) [14] knitting needles

2 #4/0 (000 or 5 mm) snaps

½ yard (45 cm) ribbon for waist sash

Small buttons for decoration, if desired

Measurements: Version A

Length from shoulder to hem	6 inches (15 cm)
Length from waist to hem	4¼ inches (11 cm)
Width around at underarm	4 inches (10 cm)
Width around at hem	10 inches (25.5 cm)
Length of sleeve seam	¾ inch (2 cm)

Measurements: Version B

Length from shoulder to hem	4 inches (10 cm)
Length from waist to hem	2½ inches (6.5 cm)
Width around at underarm	4 inches (10 cm)
Width around at hem	10 inches (25.5 cm)
Length of sleeve seam	¾ inch (2 cm)

Tension: Versions A & B

12 sts = 1 inch (2.5 cm) over st.st

14 rows = 1 inch (2.5 cm)

Abbreviation Note

sl.2tog: pass the next 2 sts on left-hand needle to right-hand needle

Instructions

Skirt

Starting at the hem, cast on 105 sts

Work 3 rows in garter sts

Version A: work the 12 rows of pattern (below) 5 times, then 1st to 6th rows 1 time

Version B: work the 12 rows of pattern (below) 2 times, then 1st to 10th rows 1 time

Pattern

1st row: k3, m1, *sl.1, k2 tog, psso, m1, k5, m1, repeat to last 6 sts, sl 1, k2 tog, psso, m1, k3

2nd & all alternate rows: purl

3rd row: k1, *k2 tog, m1, k3, m1, sl.1, k1, psso, k1, repeat from * to end

5th row: k2 tog, m1, k5, *m1, sl.1, k2 tog, psso, m1, k5, repeat from * to last 2 sts, m1, sl.1, k1, psso

7th row: sl.1, k1, psso, m1, k5, *m1, sl.2tog, k1, p2sso, m1, k5, repeat from * to last 2 sts, m1, k2 tog

9th row: k2, m1, sl.1, k1, psso, k1, k2 tog, m1, *k3, m1, sl.1, k1, psso, k1, k2 tog, m1, repeat from * to last 2 sts, k2
11th row: k3, m1, sl.1, k2 tog. psso, m1, *k5, m1, sl1, k2 tog, psso, m1, repeat from * to last 3 sts, k3
12th row: purl
Waist decrease: k2 tog (12 times), sl.1, k2 tog, psso (19 times), k2 tog (12 times), 43 sts

Bodice

Next row: k3, purl to last 3 sts, k3
Work 8 rows in st.st, keeping the k3 border at both ends of every row
Armhole Shaping
Next row: k10, cast off 2 sts, k18, cast off 2 sts, k9, turn
Back: First Side
On the last 10 sts, work 8 rows of st.st, keeping the k3 border
Neck Shaping
Cast off 5 sts, purl to end
Work 4 rows in st. st
Cast off
Top Front
Rejoin yarn to remaining sts, and work 5 rows of st.st on the 19 sts
Next row: k7, cast off 5 sts, k7
Neck Shaping: First Side
1st row: p7
2nd row: sl 1, k1, psso, k5
3rd row: p6
4th row: sl 1, k1, psso, k4
5th row: p5
Cast off
Rejoin yarn to other side of neck
Neck Shaping: Second Side
1st row: purl
2nd row: k5, k2 tog
3rd row: purl
4th row: k4, k2 tog
5th row: purl
Cast off
Back: Second Side
Rejoin yarn to remaining sts
Work 7 rows in st.st, keeping the k3 border on each row
Neck Shaping
Cast off 5 sts, knit to end
Work 5 rows in st.st
Cast off

Sleeves

Cast on 18 sts, and work 3 rows in k1, p1, rib
4th row: inc in every st. along row (36 sts)
Starting with a purl row, work 5 rows in st.st
Cast off 3 sts at beginning of next 2 rows (30 sts)
Dec 1 st at each end of next 7 rows
Cast off remaining 16 sts

To Make Up

Join shoulder seams.

Neck Edging
With right side of work facing you, pick up and knit 35 sts around the neck edge
1st row: *k1, inc3, repeat to last st, k1
Cast off
Sew sleeves in place, easing any fullness towards top of sleeve, to give a gathered puff effect. Sew up sleeve seams.

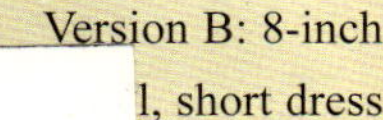
Version B: 8-inch
l, short dress

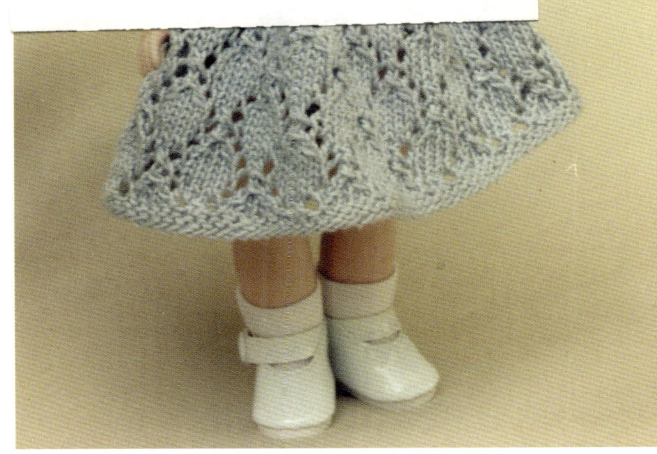

*Crocheted Dress

Betty

7½ to 8 inches (19 to 20 cm) high

A sleeveless version of this quickly crocheted frock is worn by 7½-inch Riley by Kish & Company (instructions for the matching hat can be found on page 108); short-sleeved versions with a contrasting collar are modeled both by an 8-inch Mary Englebreit's Ann Estelle by the Tonner Doll Company and by a contemporary 8-inch doll by the Alexander Doll Company.

Version A: 7½-inch doll, sleeveless dress

Materials: Version A

1 ball DMC No. 20 or DMC Cebelia No. 20 or Coats No. 20 mercer crochet cotton in main color (MC)

Small amount of contrasting color (CC), DMC or Coats No. 20

#8 US (1.25 mm) crochet hook

½ yard (50 cm) thin matching ribbon for the waist tie

3 #4/0 (000 5 mm) snaps

Materials: Version B

1 ball of DMC No. 20 or Cebelia No. 20, or Coats No. 20 mercer crochet cotton in main color (MC)

Small amount of DMC or Coats No. 20 in contrasting color (CC)

#8 US (1.25 mm) crochet hook

3 #4/0 (000 or 5 mm) snaps

1 yard (meter) thin green ribbon for collar decoration and waist tie

Measurements: Versions A & B

Length from shoulder to hem	4 inches (10 cm)
Length from waist to hem	2¼ inches (5.5 cm)
Width around at underarm	4 inches (10 cm)
Width around at hem	10 inches (25.5 cm)
Length of sleeve seam	½ inch (1.5 cm)

Tension: Versions A & B

11 dc = 1 inch (2.5 cm)

5 rows of dc = 1 inch (2.5 cm)

Instructions

Skirt

Starting at the waist, work 42 ch, miss 2 ch, turn

1st row: 1 sc in each ch, 3ch, turn (40 sc)

2nd row: 1 dc, 1 ch, 1 dc into each sc, 3 ch, turn

3rd row: *1 dc, 1 ch, 1 dc, into ch space, repeat from * to end of row, 3 ch, turn

Repeat 3rd row 9 times

13th row: 1 dc into every ch and dc

Bodice

Rejoin yarn and work 1 sc into each ch of skirt waist (40 sc), 2 ch, turn

1st row: 1 sc in each sc, 3 ch, turn

2nd row: 1 dc in each sc, 2ch, turn

3rd row: 1 sc in each dc, 3 ch, turn

Repeat 2nd & 3rd rows 1 time

Armhole Shaping

Next row: 9 dc, sl.st into the next 2 sc, 18 dc, sl.st into the next 2 sc, 9 dc, 3 ch, turn

Back: First Side

1st row: 7 dc, miss 1 dc, 1 dc in last st, 2 ch, turn

2nd row: 8 sc, turn

3rd row: slip 4 sts, 4 dc, 2 ch, turn

4th row: 4 sc, 3 ch, turn

5th row: 4 dc

Fasten off

Top Front

Miss 2 sc, rejoin yarn, 1 dc, miss 1 sc, 1 dc in the next 14 sc, miss 1 sc, 1 dc in next, 2 ch, turn

2nd row: 16 sc, 3 ch, turn

Neck Shaping: First Side

3rd row: 5 dc, 2 ch, turn

4th row: 5 sc, 3 ch, turn

5th row: 4 dc, 2 ch, turn

6th row: 4 sc, 3 ch, turn

Fasten off

Neck Shaping: Second Side

Rejoin yarn to end of cast off stitches

1st row: miss 6 sc, rejoin yarn, 5 dc, 2 ch, turn

2nd row: 5 sc, 3 ch, turn

3rd row: 4 dc, 2 ch, turn

4th row: 4 sc, 3 ch, turn

Fasten off

Back: Second Side

1st row: miss 2 sc, rejoin yarn, 9 dc, 2 ch, turn

2nd row: 7 sc, miss 1 dc, 1 sc, 3 ch, turn

3rd row: 4 dc, 2 ch, turn

4th row: 4 sc, 2 ch, turn

5th row: 4 dc

Fasten off

Note: For dolls that measure 4 inches or more around the chest, work 1 row of dc, or 2 rows of sc, up each side of back bodice opening.

Version B: 8-inch doll, short-sleeved dress with contrasting collar

Version B: Sleeves (make 2)

Using CC, work 21 ch, turn, miss 3 ch

1st row: 1 dc in each remaining ch (18 dc), 2 ch, turn

Change to MC

1st row: 1 sc in each dc, 3 ch, turn

2nd row: 1 dc in each sc, 2 ch, turn

3rd row: 1 sc in each dc, 3 ch, turn

4th row: 1 dc in each sc, 2 ch, turn

5th row: miss 1 dc, 15 sc, miss 1 dc, 1 sc in last st, 3 ch, turn

6th row: miss 1 sc, 13 dc, miss 1 sc, 1 dc in last st, 2 ch, turn

7th row: miss 1 dc, 11 sc, miss 1 dc, 1 sc in last st, 3 ch, turn

8th row: miss 1 sc, 9 dc, miss 1 sc, 1 dc in last st, 2 ch, turn

9th row: miss 1 dc, 7sc, 1 sc in last st

Fasten off

Version B: 8-inch doll, short-sleeved dress with contrasting collar

Version B: Collar (using CC, make 2)

Work 26 ch, turn, miss 2 ch

2nd row: 1 sc in each ch, (24 sc), 3 ch, turn

3rd row: 24 dc, 2 ch, turn

4th row: 24 sc, 2 ch, turn

5th row: 24 sc

Fasten off

To Make Up

Version A: Join shoulder seams. Sew up back seam to within ½-inch of waist. Fasten rest of back with snaps or Velcro. Thread fine matching ribbon through sc at waist. Make a small bow of ribbon and fasten at side of neckline.

Version B: Sew up shoulder seams, sew sleeves in place. Sew up back seam to within ½-inch of waist. Mark center of front neck. Pin collar pieces in place, from center front to back opening (omitting extra rows of dc down sides of back opening). Sew each collar in position. Thread thin ribbon through the dc rows on the collars, and sew the ribbon down at back of each collar piece.

Beverley

7½ to 8 inches (19 to 20 cm) high

All ready for the seaside in their sailor outfits are an 8-inch modern German copy of an old German celluloid doll and a 7½-inch Riley by Kish & Company. An antique 8-inch Simon & Halbig 1078 doll wears the same dress in a different color variation. (Instructions for Version A hat can be found on page 110; instructions for Version B hat can be found on page 108.)

Materials: Versions A & B

1 ball DMC No. 20 or Coats No.20 crochet cotton in main color (MC)
Small amount of No. 20 cotton in contrasting color (CC)
#8 US (1.25 mm) crochet hook
½ yard (50 cm) fine navy ribbon (red ribbon for white version)
Small amount of embroidery thread for collar decoration
2 small white star-shaped buttons for decoration at back of collar

Measurements: Versions A & B

Length from shoulder to hem	4¼ inches (10.5 cm)
Width around at underarm	4 inches (10 cm)
Width around at hem	10 inches (25 cm)
Length of sleeve seam	¾ inch (2 cm)
Length of collar from neck to hem	¾ inch (2 cm)

Tension: Versions A & B

10 sts = 1 inch (2.5 cm)
4 rows of sc and 3 rows of dc = 1 inch (2.5 cm)

Version A: 8-inch doll

Instructions

Note: the sleeves of this dress are worked as part of the main part of the bodice, beginning at the armhole shaping, with an extension on first back piece, then an extension on each side of bodice, and an extension when working second back piece. These extensions are later joined at the shoulder, thus forming the two sleeves.

Skirt

Working from the waist down and using MC, make 42 ch, turn miss 2
1st row: 1 sc in each ch to end of row (40 sc) 3 ch, turn
2nd row: 1 dc in 1st sc, *2 dc in next sc, 1 sc in next, repeat to end of row, 2 ch, turn
3rd row: 1 sc in each dc, 3 ch, turn
4th row: 1 dc in each sc, 2 ch, turn

5th row: work as 3rd row

6th row: 1 dc in each first 2 sc, *2 dc in next sc, 1 dc in each next 2 dc, repeat from * to end of row, 2 ch, turn

7th, 8th & 9th rows: work as 3rd, 4th & 5th rows

10th row: 1 dc in ea of the first 3 sc, *2 dc in next sc, 1 dc in each next 3 sc, repeat from * to end of row, 2 ch, turn

11th, 12th & 13th rows: work as 3rd, 4th & 5th rows

14th row: 1 dc in ea of first 4 sc, *2 dc in next sc, 1 dc in each of next 4 sc. repeat from * to end of row, join to top of 1st dc, 2 ch

15th row: 1 sc in each dc, 2 ch

16th row: join in CC, 2 ch, work 1 sc in each dc, 3 ch

17th row: using MC and working into back loop only of each sc, work 1 dc in each sc, 2 ch

18th row: 1 sc in each dc, 2 ch

19th row: using CC, 1 sc in each sc, 2 ch

20th row: using MC and working into back loop only of each sc, work 1 sc in each sc, 2 ch

21st row: 1 sc in each sc, working through both loops of sc in previous row

Fasten off

Version B:
8-inch doll

Bodice

1st row: return to base chain of skirt's waist, and work 1 sc in each ch (40 sc), 3 ch, turn

2nd row: 1 dc in each sc, 2 ch, turn

3rd row: 1 sc in each dc, 3 ch, turn

4th row: work as 2nd row

Divide for armholes

Back: First Side

5th row: 10 sc, 9 ch, turn, miss 3 ch (Note: 9 ch is extension for the sleeve)

6th row: 1 dc in each of next 6 ch, then 1 dc in ea of the 10 sc (16 dc), 2 ch turn

7th row: 1 sc in each dc, 2 ch, turn

8th row: 1 sc in each sc, 3 ch, turn

9th row: 1 dc in each sc, 2 ch, turn

10th & 11th rows: work as 7th & 8th rows, ending 11th row with 1 ch

Neck Shaping

12th row: slip 5 sc, 3 ch, 11 dc, 2 ch, turn

13th row: 11 sc

Fasten off

Top Front

1st row: make 8 ch, turn, miss 2 ch, 1 sc in each of the 6 ch, rejoin yarn to base of front, and work 1 sc in 20 sc across front, 9 ch, turn, miss 3 ch, 1 dc in each of next 6 ch (Note: includes sleeve extensions)

2nd row: 1 dc in each sc (32 dc) 2 ch, turn

Neck Shaping: First Side

3rd row: 16 sc, 2 ch, turn

4th row: 16 sc, 3 ch, turn

5th row: miss 1 sc, 15 dc, 2 ch, turn

6th row: 14 sc, 2 ch, turn

7th row: miss 1 st, 13 sc, 3 ch, turn

8th row: 12 dc, 2 ch, turn

9th row: miss sc 11 sc, 2 ch, turn

10th row: 10 sc

Fasten off

Neck Shaping: Second Side

Rejoin yarn to base of neck shaping at center front

1st row: 16 sc, 2 ch, turn

2nd row: 16 sc, 3 ch, turn
3rd row: 15 dc, 2 ch, turn
4th row: miss 1 sc, 14 sc, 2 ch, turn
5th row: 13 sc, 3 ch, turn
6th row: miss 1 sc, 12 dc, 2 ch, turn
7th row: 11 sc, 2 ch, turn
8th row: miss 1 sc, 10 sc
Fasten off
Back: Second Side
1st row: make 8 ch, turn, miss 2 ch, 1 sc in each 6 ch, 1 sc in 10 sc to back edge, 3 ch, turn (includes sleeve extension)
2nd row: 1 dc in each sc (16 dc), 2 ch, turn
3rd row: 1 sc in each dc, 2 ch, turn
4th row: 1 sc in each sc, 3 ch, turn
Repeat last 3 rows 1 time, ending with 1 ch on last row, turn
Neck Shaping
8th row: slip 5 sts, 1 dc in each sc, (12 dc) 2 ch, turn
9th row: 10 sc, turn, 2 ch, turn
10th row: miss 1 sc, 9 sc
Fasten off
Sew up shoulder seams

Collar

Using white cotton, make 18 ch, turn, miss 2 ch
1st row: 1 sc in each ch to end, 2 ch, turn (16 sc)
2nd row: 1 sc in each sc, 2 ch, turn
Repeat 2nd row 8 times
Divide for neck
1st row: 7 sc, 2 ch, turn
2nd row: 6 sc, 2 ch, turn
3rd row: 5 sc, 2 ch, turn
4th row: 4sc, 2 ch, turn
5th row: 4 sc, 2 ch, turn
6th row: 3 sc, 2 ch, turn
7th row: 3 sc, 2 ch, turn
8th row: 2 sc, 2 ch, turn
9th row: 2 sc, 2 ch, turn
10th row: 1 sc, 2 ch, turn
11th row: 1 sc
Chain 6
Fasten off
To make other side of collar, miss 2 sc, rejoin yarn, repeat rows 1-11 above. Chain 6. Fasten off. Sew up shoulder seams.

Contrasting Cuffs

With right side of work facing you, and using CC, work 1 row of sc (at the ends of each row) around each sleeve end. Work 1 row of sc, working into front loop of sc only in previous row. Fasten off.

To Make Up

Sew up sleeve seams. Sew up back opening to within ½ inch of waist. Sew snaps or Velcro strips down back opening.

Using navy or red embroidery cotton, work a row of stitches from the front point of the collar, down one side to 2 rows from base, then across the base, and down the other side. Sew very thin ribbon to each point of collar. Place collar on doll, and tie bow at the base of the points of the collar.

Version A: 7½-inch doll

**Crocheted Dress

Billie

8 inches (20 cm) high

Two variations of this pretty dress are modeled by a contemporary 7½-inch Ginny from the Vogue Doll Company and a 2006 doll from the Alexander Doll Company. (Instructions for the hat can be found on page 108.)

Version A:
8-inch doll

Materials: Versions A & B

1 ball DMC Babylo 10 or equivalent in main color (MC)

Small amount of DMC Babylo 10 in white or contrasting color (CC)

#8 US (1.25 mm) crochet hook

3 #4/0 (000 or 5 cm) snaps

Measurements: Versions A & B

Shoulder to hem	4 inches (10 cm)
Length from waist to hem	2½ inches (6.5 cm)
Width around at underarm	3¾ inches (9.5 cm)
Width around at hem	13½ inches (34 cm)

Tension: Versions A & B

3 patterns wide in skirt = 2 inches (5 cm)

4 pattern rows = 1 inch (2.5 cm)

Instructions

Skirt

Starting at the waist, make 38 ch, turn, miss 2 ch

1st row: work 1 sc in each of the remaining ch (36 sc), 3 ch, turn

2nd row: 2 dc in first sc, *1 dc in next sc, 3 dc in next sc, repeat from * to last sc, 1 dc, 3 ch, turn

3rd row: 5 dc in middle dc of 3 dc, *miss 1 dc, 1 dc in next dc, miss 1 dc, 5 dc in next dc, repeat from * to end of row

4th row: join in CC, 3 ch, 5 dc in middle dc of 5 dc, miss 2 dc, 1 dc in next dc, miss 2 dc, 5 dc in next, repeat to end of row. Join to 3rd ch of beginning 3 ch

5th row: using MC, 3 ch, miss 2 dc, 5 dc in next, *miss 2 dc, 1 dc in next, miss 2 dc, 5 dc in next, repeat from * to end of row, joining to top chain of first 3 ch

6th row: repeat 5th row

7th & 8th rows: repeat 4th & 5th rows

9th row: 3 ch, *miss 2 dc, 3 dc in next dc, miss 2 dc, 5 dc in next dc, repeat from * to end of row, work 2 dc in joining 3 ch, of previous row, join to top of starting ch

Fasten off

Bodice

With right side facing you, and using MC, work 1 sc in each of the beginning chain (36 ch), 2 ch, turn

2nd row: 1 sc in each sc, 2 ch, turn

Repeat last row 3 times

Back: First Side (includes armhole shaping)

8 sc, 2 ch, turn

Repeat row 5 times

7th row: 1 ch, sl.st 4 sc, then 1 sc in each next 4 sc, 2 ch, turn

8th row: 4 sc, 2 ch, turn

Repeat 8th row 1 time

Fasten off

Top Front

1st row: miss 2 sc, 2 ch, 1 sc in each next 16 sc, 2 ch, turn

2nd row: 16 sc, 2 ch, turn

Repeat last row 3 times

Neck Shaping: First Side

1st row: 4 sc, 2 ch, turn

Repeat last row 3 times

Fasten off

Neck Shaping: Second Side

Miss 8 sc, join in yarn, 2 ch, 4 sc, 2 ch, turn

Repeat last row 3 times

Fasten off

Back: Second Side (includes armhole shaping)

1st row: miss 2 sc, rejoin yarn, 1 ch, and work 1 sc in each remaining 8 sc, 2 ch, turn

2nd row: 8 sc, 2 ch, turn

Repeat last row 5 times

Neck Shaping

Next row: 4 sc, 2 ch, turn

Repeat last row 2 times

Fasten off

Sew up shoulder seams

Neck Edging

Using CC, work 1 sc in each st around neck, working 3 sc in each corner, 2 ch, turn

2nd row: 1 sc in first st, *1 picot (1 sc then 3 ch, join to top of sc), 1 sc in next, repeat from * around neck

Version B: 7½-inch doll

To Make Up

Sew up back seam from hem to top contrast row. Sew on snaps to close back opening.

Note: for a chubbier doll, work 2 rows of sc down each side of back opening to waist.

**Knitted Dress with Contrasting Sleeves and Neck Insert

Blanche

7½ to 8 inches (19 to 20 cm) high

This very versatile dress can be made to wear alone, as modeled by 7½-inch Riley by Kish & Company and by an 8-inch doll by the Alexander Doll Company, or as a pinafore frock, to be worn with a blouse from Chapter 4, as seen on an 8-inch Mary Englebreit's Ann Estelle by the Tonner Doll Company.

Version A: 8-inch doll, dress with collar and sleeves

Materials: Versions A & B

1 ball DMC Babylo 10 or equivalent in main color (MC)

Small amount of DMC Babylo 10 in white or contrasting color (CC)

#0 US (2 mm) [14] knitting needles

Small length of narrow ribbon for neck trim

3 #4/0 (000 or 5 mm) snaps

Measurements: Versions A & B

Shoulder to hem	3¾ inches (9.5 cm)
Waist to hem	2¼ inches (6 cm)
Width around at underarm	4 inches (10 cm)
Width around at hem	7½ inches (19 cm)
Length of sleeve seam	¾ inch (2 cm)

Tension: Versions A & B

11 sts = 1 inch (2.5 cm)

14 rows = 1 inch (2.5 cm)

Version B: 8-inch doll, sleeveless pinafore

Instructions

Skirt

Starting at the hem, cast on 84 sts
1st row: knit
2nd row: purl
3rd row: *p1, k5, repeat to end of row
4th row: k1, *p3, k3 repeat to last 5 st, p3, k2
5th row: p3, *k1, p5, repeat to last 3 sts, k1, p2
6th row: knit
7th row: p3, *k1, p5, repeat to last 3 sts, k1, p2
8th row: k1, *p3, k3, repeat to last 5 sts, p3, k2
9th row: p1, k5, repeat to end of row
10th row: purl
Work 24 rows in st.st, starting with a knit row
Waist decrease row: k2 tog, all along row
Next row: cast on 2 st, purl to end of row, cast on 2 sts
Work 10 rows in st.st
Armhole and Neck Shaping
1st row: k11, cast off 3, k5, cast off 6, k5, cast off 3, k10
Back: First Side
Keeping the 2 st garter sts border, and beginning with a purl row, work 8 rows on the first 11 sts
Neck Shaping
Next row: cast off 5 sts, work to end
Work 2 rows in st.st
Cast off remaining sts
Top Front: First Side
Rejoin yarn, and starting with a purl row, work 10 rows st.st on the 6 sts
Cast off
Top Front: Second Side
Rejoin yarn and starting with a purl row, work 10 rows on the 6 sts
Cast off
Back: Second Side
Rejoin yarn, beginning with a purl row, and keeping the 2 st garter st border work 7 rows
Neck Shaping
Cast off 5 sts, work to end
Work 3 rows
Cast off remaining sts

Version A: Sleeves (make 2)

Using MC, cast on 14 sts
Knit 2 rows
Change to white or CC
Next row: incl st in every st (28 sts)
Work 5 rows in st.st beginning with a purl row
Sleeve Top Shaping
Cast off 3 sts at beginning of next 6 rows
Cast off remaining 10 sts

Version A: Collar (make 2)

Using white or CC, cast on 16 sts
Knit 2 rows
Purl 1 row
Knit 1 row
Repeat last 2 rows 1 time
Cast off

Version A: Neck Insert

Using white or CC, cast on 9 sts
Work 6 rows in st.st
Cast off

To Make Up

Version A: Iron with a warm iron. Sew up shoulder seams. Carefully sew front insert into front neck. Sew in sleeves. Sew up sleeve seams. Sew up back seam from hem to within ¾-inch of waist. Sew on snaps to close back opening. Trim with a matching color bow at neck.

Version B: Iron with a warm iron. Sew up shoulder seams. Sew up back seam from hem to within ¾-inch of waist. Sew on snaps to close back opening.

Version A: 7½-inch doll, dress with collar and sleeves

*Crocheted Dress

Briony

8 inches (20 cm) high

A quick crocheter can make this charming dress in one evening. It is modeled in two variations: by 8-inch Dru from the Tonner Doll Company and by an 8-inch doll from the Alexander Doll Company. The skirt can be made shorter or longer by working more or less rows.

Version A:
8-inch doll,
solid-color dress

Materials: Version A

1 ball No. 8 mercerized crochet cotton or equivalent
#8 US (1.25 mm) crochet hook
3 #4/0 (000 or 5 mm) snaps
Small buttons for decoration

Materials: Version B

1 ball Perle No. 8 crochet cotton (cheaper variety is softer to touch when finished)
Small amount No. 8 mercerized crochet cotton for edge of collar
#8 US (1.25 mm) crochet hook
3 #4/0 (000 or 5 mm) snaps
Small buttons for decoration

Measurements	**Version A**	**Version B**
Shoulder to hem	4 inches (10 cm)	4¼ inches (11 cm)
Waist to hem	2¼ inches (5.5 cm)	2¼ inches (5.5 cm)
Width around at underarm	3½ inches (9 cm)	4 inches (10 cm)
Width around hem	9 inches (23 cm)	10 inches (25.5 cm)

Tension: Version A

11 dc = 1 inch (2.5 cm)
11 rows of skirt pattern = 2 inches (5 cm)

Tension: Version B

10 dc = 1 inch (2.5 cm)
10 rows of skirt pattern = 2 inches (5 cm)

Instructions

Skirt

Starting at the waist, work 44 ch, turn, miss 2 ch
1st row: 1 sc in each chain (42 sc), 3 ch, turn
2nd row: *6 dc, 2 dc in next sc, repeat from * to end of row (48 dc) 3 ch, turn
3rd row: 1 dc, then 5 dc (shell) in next dc, *miss 1 dc, 1 sc in next, miss 1 dc, 5 dc (shell) in next, repeat from * to last st, 1 dc, 3 ch, turn
4th row: *5 dc into 3rd dc of shell, 1 dc in sc, repeat from * to end of row, 3 ch, turn
5th row: 5 dc into 3rd dc of shell, *2 dc into 1 dc, 5 dc into 3rd dc of shell, repeat from * to last st, 1 dc in last st, join to top of turning 3 ch at beginning of row
6th round: 3 ch, 5 dc into 3rd dc of shell, * 3 dc in space between the 2 dc in previous row, 5dc into 3rd dc of shell, repeat from * to last st., 1 dc, join to 3rd ch at beginning of row

7th round: 3 ch, 5 dc into 3rd dc of shell, *4 dc into center dc of 3 dc group, 5 dc into 3rd dc of shell, repeat from * to last st, 1 dc, join to top ch of 3ch
8th round: 3 ch, 1 dc, 5 dc into 3rd dc of shell *4 dc into space between 3nd and 4th dc of group, 5 dc into 3rd dc of shell, repeat from * to last st, 1 dc, join to top ch of 3 ch
Repeat 8th round 5 times
Fasten off

Bodice

Rejoin yarn to waist and starting with 2 ch, work 1 sc into each of the original chain sts (42 sc) 2 ch, turn
2nd row: 1 sc in each sc, 2 ch, turn
3rd row: 1 sc in each sc, 3 ch, turn
4th row: 1 dc in each sc, 1 ch, turn
5th row: 1 sc in each dc, 1 ch, turn
6th row: 1 sc in each sc, 1 ch, turn
7th row: 1 sc in each sc, 3 ch, turn
8th row: 1 dc in each sc, 1 ch, turn
Divide for armholes
9th row: 9 sc, 1 ch, turn
Back: First Side
10th row: sl 1 sc, 8 sc, 1 ch, turn
11th row: sl 3 sc, 2 ch, 5 dc, 2 ch, turn
Neck Shaping
12th row: 5 sc, 3 ch, turn
13th row: 5 sc
Fasten off
Top Front
1st row: miss 3 dc, 1 ch, 1 sc in next 18 ch, turn
2nd row: 2 ch, 18 sc
3rd row: repeat 2nd row
Neck Shaping: First Side
4th row: 3 ch, 5 dc
**Next 3 rows: 2 ch, 5 sc
Fasten off**
Neck Shaping: Second Side
1st row: miss 8 sc, 3 ch, 5 dc, then work from ** to ** to finish
Back: Second Side
1st row: miss 3 ch, 9 sc, 3 ch, turn
2nd row: 9 dc, 3 ch, turn
Neck Shaping
3rd row: 5 dc, 2 ch, turn
4th row: 5 sc, 2 ch, turn
5th row: repeat 4th row
Fasten off
Sew up shoulder seams

Collar

With wrong side of work facing you,
1st row: 3 ch, 1 dc into each 4 sc of back neck shaping, 3 dc in corner, 11 dc along edge of shoulder, 3 dc in corner, 8 dc along front neck shaping, 3 dc in corner, 11 dc along edge of shoulder, 3 dc in corner, 4 dc
2nd row: 3 ch, 5 dc, 3 dc in middle of 3 dc cluster, 13 dc over shoulder, 3 dc in middle of cluster, 10 dc across neck, 3 dc in cluster, 13 dc over shoulder, 3 dc in cluster, 5 dc
3rd row: 3 ch, *miss 1 dc, 5 dc in next dc, repeat to last stitch
Fasten off

To Make Up

Fold collar over to front, attach end of collar to corresponding edge of back. Sew tiny buttons on one side, use dc rows on other side for buttonholes, or close opening with snaps. Decorate corners of collar with fancy buttons.

Version B: 8-inch doll, dress with contrasting decoration

**Knitted Striped Dress

Bronwyn

8 inches (20 cm) high

Two contemporary 8-inch dolls by the Alexander Doll Company wear striking striped dresses in different color combinations.

Version A: 8-inch doll, yellow, pink and navy combination

Materials: Versions A & B

1 ball DMC Perle No. 5 or Pelicano No. 5 by Coats or equivalent in main color (MC) Version A: yellow; Version B: white

1 ball DMC Perle No. 5, or Pelicano No. 5 by Coats or equivalent in 1st contrasting color (1CC) Version A: dark pink: Version B: red

1 ball DMC Perle No. 5 or Pelicano No. 5 by Coats or equivalent in 2nd contrasting color (2CC) Versions A & B: navy

#1 US (2.25 mm) [13] knitting needles

3 4/0 (000 or 5 mm) snaps

Stick-on diamantes for decoration

½ yard (meter) ribbon for belt

1 small buckle

Measurements: Versions A & B

Length from shoulder to hem	4¼ inches (11 cm)
Length from waist to hem	2½ inches (6.5 cm)
Width around at underarm	5 inches (12.5 cm)

Tension: Versions A & B

10 sts = 1 inch (2.5 cm)

18 rows = 1 inch (skirt)

Instructions

Skirt, worked sideways in garter st (make 2)
With 2CC, cast on 22 sts
1st row: knit with 2CC
2nd & 3rd rows: knit with 1CC
4th & 5th rows: knit with MC
6th & 7th rows: knit with 2CC
Repeat last 6 rows 9 times (30 ribs)
Cast off

Bodice

Using MC, pick up and knit 26 sts along one side of one piece of skirt
Using MC, work 6 rows of garter st
Armhole Shaping
Cast off 4 sts at beg of next 2 rows (18 sts)
Knit 8 rows
Neck Shaping: First Side
1st row: k6, cast off 6 sts, k5
2nd row: k4, k2 tog
Knit 3 rows
Cast off
Neck Shaping: Second Side
Rejoin yarn to side of neck
1st row: k2 tog, k4
Knit 3 rows

Version B: 8-inch doll, white, red and navy combination

Cast off
Back: Right Side
Using MC, with right side of remaining skirt piece facing you, pick up and knit 13 sts along one edge
Knit 7 rows
Armhole Shaping
Cast off 2 sts at beg of next row
Knit 10 rows
Neck Shaping
Cast off 6 sts, knit to end
Knit 4 rows on remaining sts
Cast off
Back: Left Side
Join in MC yarn beside the bottom of the Back Right Side, pick up 13 sts along end of skirt rows
Knit 6 rows
Armhole Shaping
Cast off 2 sts
Knit 10 rows
Neck Shaping
Cast off 6 sts, knit to end
Work 4 rows
Cast off
Sew up shoulder seams

Neckband

Using 2CC, pick up 29 sts around neck, omitting 2 sts at both edges of back opening
1st row: knit with 2CC
2nd row: Using 1CC, *k1, inc3 (by knitting into the front, then the back and then the front again of the next st), repeat from * to end of row
3rd row: Using 1CC, knit 1 row
Cast off loosely using 1CC

Armhole Bands

Using 2CC, pick up and knit 21 sts around one armhole
Work 3 rows as in neckband
Cast off loosely
Work other armhole in the same way

To Make Up

Sew up side seams. Sew on snaps to close back opening. Decorate with fancy buttons or stick-on diamantes. Place buckle on ribbon, center buckle at middle of front, and stitch in place. Anchor ribbon at each side seam with 2 small stitches, and then make a bow at center back with remaining ribbon.

Chapter 3

Skirts

These skirts come in different waist sizes. Most can be altered by using elastic to fit the waist of a particular doll. Several of the following patterns also include instructions as to where to shorten or lengthen the pattern to suit the height of the doll.

**Knitted July 4th or Western Skirt

Caroline

3¼- to 3½-inch (8½- to 9-cm) waist

This very versatile skirt is knitted sideways for the main part, with the decorative hem section worked lengthwise and added afterwards. Thus the skirt can be made with or without the decorative hem, and in other color variations.

Version A: July 4th Motif

Materials: Version A

1 ball Sullivan or Milford soft knitting cotton (equal to 4 ply) or equivalent in blue (MC)
Small amount of Sullivan or Milford soft knitting cotton in red (1CC)
Small amount of Sullivan or Milford soft knitting cotton in white (2CC)
#1 US (2.25 mm) [13] knitting needles
#0 US (2 mm) [14] knitting needles
1 #4/0 (000 or 5mm) snaps
8 small white star-shaped buttons for decoration
Length of thin elastic, if needed

Materials: Version B

1 ball Sullivan or Milford soft knitting cotton (equal to 4 ply) or equivalent in main color (MC)
Small amount Sullivan or Milford soft knitting cotton in brown (1CC)
Small amount of Sullivan or Milford soft knitting cotton in cream (2CC)
Small amount of Sullivan or Milford soft knitting cotton in orange (3CC)
#0 US (2 mm) [14] knitting needles
1 #4/0 (000 or 5mm) snap
Length of thin elastic, if needed

Measurements	**Version A**	**Version B**
Length from waist to hem	3½ inches (9 cm)	2 7/8 inches (7 cm)
Width around at waist	3½ inches (9 cm)	3¼ inches (8.5 cm)
Width around at hem	8 inches (20 cm)	8½ inches (21.5 cm)

Tension: Version A	**Version B**
8 sts = 1 inch (2.5 cm)	9 sts = 1 inch (2.5 cm)
10 rows = 1 inch (2.5 cm)	12 rows = 1 inch (2.5 cm)

Instructions

Skirt (worked sideways)

Pattern

Using #1 US (2.25 mm) [13] needles, cast on 21 sts

1st row: knit 21

2nd row: p18, wl fwd, sl 1, turn

3rd row: wl bk, sl 1 st, k18

4th row: p18, k3

For a slim doll, with a 3- 3½-inch waist, repeat the 4 rows of pattern 16-17 times.

For a chubbier doll, such as an 8-inch Alexander doll, repeat the 4 rows of pattern 20 times.

Cast off

Note: the skirt can be left at this length (see To Make Up) or can be lengthened by adding the hem border, below.

Hem Border

Version A: Using #0 US (2 mm) [14] needles and MC, pick up and knit 70 sts along the long side edge of the skirt

2nd row: purl, end off

3rd row: using white yarn (2CC), knit 1 row

4th row: change to red yarn (1CC), work 4 rows in st.st, beginning with a knit row, end off yarn

8th & 9th rows: using white yarn, knit these 2 rows, fasten off yarn

10th - 13th rows: using (MC), work these 4 rows in st.st, beginning with a knit row

Cast off using the purl st

Version B: Using first contrasting color (1CC), pick up and knit 82 sts along the long side edge of skirt

2nd row: knit using 1CC, break off yarn, join in second contrasting color (2CC)

3rd row: using 2CC, knit

4th row: * using third contrasting color (3CC), p1, p5 (2CC), repeat from to last 4 sts, p1 (3CC), p3 (2CC)

5th row: k2 (2CC), *k3 (3CC), k3 (2CC) repeat from * to end of row

6th row: work as 3rd row

7th row: work as 2nd row, break off 2CC and 3CC, join in 1CC

8th row: using 1CC, purl

9th row: repeat 7th row

Cast off using a purl st

To Make Up

Versions A & B

Sew up back seam (from hem) to ½-inch from top. Close with a snap. Version A: Decorate the red band with white star-shaped buttons.

Version B:
Western Motif

*Knitted Halloween or High Fashion Skirt

Casey

3½-inch (9-cm) waist

Version A, modeled by an 8-inch Betsy McCall by the Tonner Doll Company, was originally designed as part of a Halloween outfit, but the skirt is very versatile and can be made in any color and yarn of your choice, as seen in Version B, which can be made as part of a High Fashion outfit.

Version A: Halloween

Version B: High Fashion

Materials: Version A

1 ball DMC or Coats No. 20 mercer crochet cotton or equivalent

#0 US (2 mm) [14] knitting needles

1 #4/0 (000 or 5 mm) snap or short length of thin elastic

Materials: Version B

1 ball of DMC Babylo 10 or equivalent (MC)

Small amount of DMC Babylo 10 or equivalent in white or contrasting color (CC)

#0 US (2 mm) [14] knitting needles

1 #4/0 (000 or 5 mm) snap or short length of thin elastic

Measurements:	**Version A**	**Version B**
Length from waist to hem	2¾ inches (7 cm)	2¾ inches (7 cm)
Width around waist	3½ inches (9 cm)	3½ inches (9 cm)
Width around hem	9½ inches (24 cm)	10 inches (25.5 cm)

Tension: Version A	**Version B**
12 sts = 1 inch (2.5 cm)	12 sts = 1 inch (2.5cm)
14 rows = 1 inch (2.5 cm)	15 rows = 1 inch (2.5 cm)

Instructions

Starting at the hem, cast on 109 sts

Version A: Work 6 rows in ms.st, k2 tog at end of 6th row

Version B: Using CC, work 4 rows in ms.st, change to MC

Work 4 rows in st.st, starting with a knit row, and p2 tog at end of 4th row

Versions A & B

1st decrease row: k8, (k2 tog, k16) 5 times, k2 tog, k8

Work 1 row purl, 1 row knit, 1 row purl

2nd decrease row: k7, (k2 tog, k15) 5 times, k2 tog, knit to end

Work 3 rows in st.st

3rd decrease row: k6, (k2 tog k14) 5 times, k 2 tog, knit to end

Work 5 rows in st.st

4th decrease row: k5, (k2 tog, k13) 5 times, k2 tog, knit to end

Work 5 rows in st.st

5th decrease row: k4, (k2 tog, k12) 5 times, k2 tog, knit to end

Work 5 rows in st.st

Next row: k2 tog, repeat all along row

Work 4 rows of k1, p1 rib

Cast off loosely

To Make Up

Sew up back seam from hem to within 1 inch of waist. Fasten with a snap or, if needed, sew up complete seam and then thread elastic through rib at waist.

Charlotte

3- to 4-inch (7.5- to 10-cm) waist

Because this skirt is worked sideways, this is a very versatile pattern. By using different yarns, you can create very different finished skirts, which can be lengthened by using more stitches. This skirt can easily be made to fit any size waist by adding or subtracting the number of rows worked.

Materials: Version A (not pictured)
1 ball of DMC Perle No. 8 or equivalent
#8 US (1.25 mm) crochet hook
Small hook & eye or length of thin elastic

Materials: Version B
½ spool Cameo yarn (used for punch embroidery)
#8 US (1.25 mm) crochet hook
Small hook & eye or length of thin elastic

Materials: Version C
½ ball DMC Babylo 10 or equivalent
#8 US (1.25 mm) crochet hook
1 #4/0 (000 or 5 mm) snap or length of thin elastic

Materials: Version D
1 ball of DMC Perle No. 5, or Pelicano No. 5 or equivalent
#8 US (1.25 mm) steel or aluminum crochet hook
1 #4/0 (000 or 5 mm) snap or a length of thin elastic

Version B

Measurements	**Version A**	**Version B**	**Version C**	**Version D**
Length from waist to hem	2¼ inches (6 cm)	2½ inches (6.5 cm)	2½ inches (6.5 cm)	2¾ inches (7 cm)
Width around waist	3½ inches (8 cm)	3½ inches (8 cm)	4 inches (10 cm)	4 inches (10 cm)
Width around hem	5½ inches (14 cm)	5 inches (13 cm)	7½ inches (19 cm)	7½ inches (19 cm)

Tension: **Version A**
12 dc = 1 inch (2.5 cm)
4 rows dc & 4 rows sc = 1 inch (2.5 cm)

Version B
10 dc = 1 inch (2.5 cm)
4 rows sc & 3 rows dc = 1 inch (2.5 cm)

Version C
10 dc = 1 inch (2.5 cm)
4 sc rows & 3 dc rows = 1 inch (2.5 cm)

Version D
9 dc = 1 inch (2.5 cm)
3 sc rows & 3 dc rows = 1 inch (2.5 cm)

Instructions

Note: all versions are worked sideways from one back edge to the other back edge.

Versions A & B

Starting at the back edge, work 23 ch, turn, miss 3 ch

1st row: 15 dc, 5 sc, 2 ch, turn

2nd row: 20 sc, 2 ch, turn

Repeat last 2 rows 19 times

Fasten off

Version C & D

Note: all sc rows worked on Version C (red skirt) are worked through the back thread only of each sc st, which creates a different ribbed effect.

Work 24 ch, turn, miss 2 ch

1st row: 22 sc, 3 ch, turn

2nd row: 16 sc, 3 hdc, 3 sc, 2 ch, turn

Repeat last 2 rows 19 times (can be lengthened if required)

Waistband (same for all versions)

Work 40 sc along short side of skirt

Next row: 2 ch, 40 sc

Repeat last row

Fasten off

To Make Up

Sew up the back seam to within ½-inch of waistband. Either thread thin elastic through sc at waist, or attach a snap or hook & eye to fasten waistband.

Version C

Version D

Cheryl

2½-inch (6.5-cm) waist

Because of the way this skirt is knitted, it not only has the appearance of a wide flared skirt, but also has a lovely pleated effect.

Materials

½ ball DMC Babylo 10 or equivalent
#0 US (2 mm) [14] knitting needles
Small hook & eye or length of thin elastic

Measurements

Waist to hem	2½ inches (6.5 cm)
Width around waist	3¾ inches (9.5 cm)
Width around hem (un-extended)	8½ inches (21.5 cm)
Width around hem (extended)	10 inches (25.5 cm)

Tension

Bottom of one panel (10 sts) = ¾ inch (2 cm)
Top of one panel (4 sts) = 3/8 inch (1 cm)
14 rows = 1 inch (2.5 cm)

Instructions

Starting at the hem, cast on 122 sts
Start by working on the wrong side first
1st row: (wrong side of work) *k2, p10, repeat from * to last 2 sts, k2
2nd row: *p2, k4, sl.1, k5, repeat from * to last 2 sts, p2
Repeat these 2 rows 2 times, then repeat 1st row 1 time
8th row: *p2, k4, sl.1, k2 tog, k3, repeat from * to last 2 sts, p2
9th row: *k2, p9, repeat from * to last 2 sts, k2
10th row: *p2, k4, sl.1, k4, repeat from * to last 2 sts, p2
Repeat last 2 rows 2 times, then repeat 9th row 1 time
16th row: *p2, k2, k2 tog, sl.1, k4, repeat from * to last 2 sts, p2
17th row: *k2, p8, repeat from * to last 2 sts, k2
18th row: *p2, k3, sl.1, k4, repeat from * to last 2 st, p2
Repeat last 2 rows 1 time, then 17th row 1 time
22nd row: *p2, k3, sl.1, k2 tog, p2, repeat from * to last 2 sts, p2
23rd row: *k2, p7, repeat from * to last 2 sts, k2
24th row: *p2, k3, sl.1, k3, repeat from * to last 2 sts, p2
Repeat last 2 rows 1 time, then repeat 23rd row 1 time
28th row: *p2, k1, k2 tog, sl.1, k3, repeat from * to last 2 sts, p2
29th row: *k2, p6, repeat from * to last 2 sts, k2
30th row: *p2, k2, sl.1, k3, repeat from * to last 2 sts, p2
Repeat last 2 rows 1 time, then repeat 29th row again
34th row: *p2, k2, sl.1, k2 tog, k1, repeat from * to last 2 sts, p2
35th row: *k2, p5, repeat from * to last 2 sts, k2
36th row: *p2, k2, sl.1, k2 repeat from * to last 2 sts, p2
Repeat last 2 rows 1 time, then repeat 35th row 1 time
40th row: *p2, k2 tog, sl.1, k2 repeat from * to last 2 sts, p2
41st row: *k2, p4, repeat from * to last 2 sts, k2
42nd row: *p2, k1, sl.1, k2, repeat from * to last 2 sts, k2
Repeat last 2 rows 1 time, then repeat 41st row 1 time
46th row: *p2 tog, k1, sl.1, k2 tog, repeat to the last 2 sts, p2 tog
47th row: *k1, p3, repeat from * to the last st, k1
Work 3 rows in k1, p1, rib
Cast off

To Make Up

Sew up back seam to within ½-inch of ribbed waistband. Either join with a hook & eye, or thread elastic through waist to fit doll.

Chapter 4

Sweaters and Blouses

When making sweaters or blouses, whether knitted or crocheted, remember that even dolls that are the same height may have arms of different lengths. Long sleeves can be lengthened or shortened to suit each doll. The patterns in this chapter include plain and fancy styles; two feature a faux-cable pattern. By mixing and matching each top with different skirts, slacks and shorts you can create a wide variety of outfits.

***Knitted Faux-Cable Sweater

Dahlia

7½ to 9 inches (19 to 23 cm) high

With a simple faux-cable pattern and either long or short sleeves, this sweater can be worn by a variety of dolls, including a 9-inch doll by the Lawton Doll Company, a 7½-inch Riley by Kish & Company and an 8-inch Dru by Tonner Doll Company.

Version 1A: 9-inch doll

Materials: Version A (long sleeves)
Small ball of 2 ply wool/yarn or equivalent
#0 US (2mm) [14] knitting needles
2 #4/0 (000 or 5 mm) snaps

Materials: Version B (short sleeves)
1 ball DMC Babylo 10 or equivalent
#0 US (2 mm) [14] knitting needles
2 #4/0 (000 or 5 mm) snaps

Measurements: Version A

Length from shoulder to hem	2½ inches (6.5 cm)
Width around at underarm	4½ inches (11.5 cm)
Length of sleeve seam	1¾ inches (4.5 cm)

Measurements: Version B

Length from shoulder to hem	2½ inches (6.5 cm)
Width around at underarm	4 inches (10 cm)
Length of sleeve seam	½ inch (1.5 cm)

Tension: long sleeves
12 sts of pattern = 1 inch (2.5 cm)
14 rows = 1 inch (2.5 cm)

Tension: short sleeves
12 sts of pattern = 1 inch (2.5 cm)
14 rows = 1 inch (2.5 cm)

Abbreviation Note
Twist: knit into front of 2nd st on left-hand needle, then into front of first st on needle.

Instructions

Back

Cast on 28 st and work 5 rows in k1, p1 rib, inc. 1 st at end of last row

1st row: p1 *k2, p3, repeat from * to last 3 sts, k2, p1

Pattern

2nd row: k1 p2, *k3, p2 repeat from * to last 3 sts, p2, k1

3rd row: p1, *twist2, p3, repeat from * to last 3 sts, twist2, p1

Version A: repeat last 2 rows 5 times

Version B: repeat last 2 rows 4 times

Divide for back and armholes

Back: First Side

Cast off 3 sts, work 11 sts in pattern (include st on needle after casting off), cast on 2 sts for underlap

Work 10 rows in pattern, working the 2 extra sts in garter st in each row

Neck Shaping

Cast off 2 sts at neck edge in next row

Work 1 row

Work 2 sts tog at neck edge on next and alternate rows 1 time

Cast off

Back: Second Side

Rejoin yarn and cast on 2 sts for the overlap

1st row: work in pattern to end

Work 9 rows in pattern, working the 2 extra sts in garter sts

Neck Shaping

Cast off 3 sts at back opening end, work in pattern to end of row

Work 1 row

Work 2 sts tog at neck edge on next and alternate row

Cast off

Front

Cast on 28 sts and work 5 rows in k1, p1 rib, inc 1 st at end of last row

1st row: p1, *k2, p3, repeat from * to last 3 sts, k2, p1

2nd row: k1, *p2, k3, repeat from * to last 3 sts, p2, k1

3rd row: p1 *twist2, p3, repeat from * to last 3 sts, twist2, p1

Version A: repeat last 2 rows 5 times

Version B: repeat last 2 rows 4 times

Versions A & B

Armhole Shaping

Keeping pattern as set, cast off 3 sts at beginning of next 2 rows

Cast off 1 st at beginning of next 4 rows

Work 6 rows in pattern

Neck Shaping: First Side

Work 8 sts, cast off 3 sts, work to end of row

Working on the last 8 sts

1st row: work in pattern to last 2 sts, p2 tog

2nd row: k2 tog, work to end row

3rd row: work to last 2 sts, k2 tog

Work 3 rows on these 5 sts

Cast off

Neck Shaping: Second Side

Rejoin to other side of neck

1st row: p2 tog, work in pattern to end

2nd row: work in pattern to last 2 sts, k2 tog

3rd row: k2 tog, work in pattern to end

Version 2A: 7½-inch doll

Work 3 rows
Cast off

Version A: Long Sleeves (make 2)

Version A: cast on 18 sts
Work 5 rows in k1, p1, rib, inc 1 st at end of last row
Work in pattern as given for 8 rows
9th row: keeping to pattern inc1 st. at both ends of row
Work 5 rows in pattern
15th row: repeat 9th row
Work 5 rows in pattern
21st row: repeat 9th row (25 sts)
Work 3 rows
Sleeve Top Shaping
Dec 1 st at each end of every row, until 7 sts remain
Cast off

Version B: Short Sleeves (make 2)

Cast on 18 sts
Work 3 rows in k1, p1 rib, increasing 1 st at end of last row
1st row: p1, *k2, p3, repeat from * to last 3 sts, k2, p1
2nd row: inc in 1st st, *p2, k3, repeat from * to last 3 sts, p2, inc. in last st (21 sts)
3rd row: p2, *twist, p3, repeat from * to last 4 sts, twist, p2
4th row: inc, k1, *p2, k3, repeat from * to last 4 sts, p2, k1, inc in last st (23 sts)
5th row: p3, *twist, p3, repeat from * to last 5 sts, twist, p3
6th row: k3, *p2, k3, repeat from * to last 5 sts, p2 k3
Sleeve Top Shaping
Dec 1 st at each end of next row
Work 1 row
Dec at each end of every row until 7 sts remain
Cast off remaining sts

To Make Up

Sew up shoulder seams. Pick up and knit 34 sts around neck. Work 2 rows in k1 p1 rib. Cast off loosely in rib. Sew sleeves into armholes, sew up sleeve seams and side seams. Close back opening with snaps.

Version B: 8-inch doll

Danielle

8 to 9 inches (20 to 23 cm) high

A 9-inch composition look-a-like Patsy and an 8-inch doll by the Alexander Doll Company model their two-toned sweaters.

Materials: Version A
1 ball Semco/Milford/Coats or Sullivan soft knitting cotton (equivalent to 4 ply) in main color (MC)
Small amount of Milford or Sullivan soft knitting cotton in contrasting color (CC)
#1 US (2.25 mm) [13] knitting needles
3 #4/0 (000 or 5 mm) snaps

Materials: Version B
1 ball of DMC Perle No. 5 or Pelicano No. 5 (or equivalent) in main color (3 ply yarn can be used) (MC)
Small amount of DMC Perle No. 5 or Pelicano No. 5 in contrasting color (CC)
#0 US (2 mm) [14] knitting needles
3 #4/0 (000 or 5 mm) snaps

Measurements	**Version A**	**Version B**
Length for shoulder to hem	2¾ inches (7 cm)	2½ inches (6.5 cm)
Width around at underarm	5 inches (12.5 cm)	4 inches (10 cm)
Length of sleeve seam	1¾ inches (4.5 cm)	1¼ inches (3 cm)

Tension: Version A	**Version B**
8 sts = 1 inch (2.5 cm)	10 sts = 1 inch (2.5cm)
11 rows = 1 inch (2.5 cm)	12 rows = 1 inch (2.5cm)

Version A: 9-inch doll

Instructions

Front

***For both Version A and B work in st.st throughout, and using equivalent knitting needles, cast on 22 sts with MC
Work 3 rows in k1, p1, rib
Work 2 rows in st.st

Pattern
1st row: *k1 CC, k1 MC, repeat from * to end of row
2nd row: *p1 CC, p1 MC, repeat from * to end of row
3rd row: repeat 1st row
4th row: purl MC
5th row: knit MC
6th row: *p1 MC, p1 CC, repeat from * to end of row
7th row: *k1 MC, k1 CC, repeat from * to end of row
8th row: repeat 6th row
Armhole Shaping
9th row: cast off 2 sts at beginning of next 2 rows***
10th row: Keeping continuity of pattern, work 7 rows in pattern as set
Neck Shaping
11th row: p7, cast off 4 sts loosely, p7
Version A
***12th & 13th rows: dec 1 st at neck edge

14th row: work 1 row in st.st
Cast off remaining sts***
Neck Shaping: Second Side
Repeat from *** to ***
Version B
12th & 13th rows: dec 1 st at neck edge
14th & 15th rows: keeping continuity of pattern, work in st.st
Cast off remaining sts
Neck Shaping: Second Side
Repeat 12th to 15th rows
Cast off

Work other side of neck to match

Back: First Side

Version A: Work as for front to ***, keeping continuity of pattern as set

Version B:
8-inch doll

Version B: Working in MC throughout
Work 8 rows of st.st
Cast off 2 sts at beginning of next 2 rows
Versions: A & B
1st row: k2 tog, work 7 sts, cast on 2 sts for under lap
2nd row: k2, purl to end
Work 11 rows as set, keeping garter st border
Neck Shaping
1st row: Cast off 5 sts, work to end of row
2nd row: knit, k2 tog at end of row
3rd row: p2 tog, purl to end
Cast off remaining sts

Back: Second Side

Version A: rejoin yarn, and work other side of back to suit, leaving out the 2 st border of garter sts
Version B: rejoin yarn, cast on 2 sts for under lap, work to end of row, k2 tog
Versions A & B: work 11 rows in st.st
Neck Shaping
Cast off 5 st, work to end of row
Purl 1 row
Next row k2 tog, knit to end of row
Purl 1 row
Cast off remaining sts

Long Sleeves (make 2)

Starting at the wrist, and using MC, cast on 14 sts
Work 3 rows in k1, p1 rib
Work 5 rows in st.st
Inc1 st. at each end of next row
Work 5 rows in st.st
Inc 1 st at each end of next row
Work 2 rows in st.st
Sleeve Shaping
Continuing in st.st, cast off 2 sts at beg of next 2 rows
Dec 1 st at each end of next knit row and every following knit row until 4 sts remain
Cast off remaining sts

To Make Up

Sew up shoulder seams. Sew in sleeves, sew up sleeve and side seams. Using MC, with right side of work facing you, pick up 30 sts around neck edge. Work 2 rows in k1, p1 rib. Cast off. Use snaps to close back opening.

Daphne

8 to 9 inches (20 to 23 cm) high

A 9-inch wooden doll by Raikes Collectibles (Version 1A) and an 8-inch vinyl doll from the 1970s (Version 2A) both wear sweaters with a knitted-in decoration at the front yoke. Two 8-inch 2006 dolls by the Alexander Doll Company wear the same sweaters, but one is plain and opens in front (Version 1B), while the other has a back opening and a design worked in cross stitch, using the stitches as a base, on the front (Version 2B).

Materials: Version A

½ ball of DMC Perle No. 5, or Pelicano No. 5 yarn (MC)

Small amount of DMC Perle No. 5, or Peluicano No. 5 yarn in contrasting color (CC)

#1 US (2.25 mm) [13] knitting needles

1 #4/0 (000 or 5 mm) snap

Materials: Version B

1 ball Sullivan or Milford soft knitting cotton (equal to 4 ply) or equivalent (MC)

#0 US (2 mm) [14] knitting needles

1 #4/0 (000 or 5mm) snap

Optional: DMC embroidery yarn in colors of your choice

Measurements: Version A

Shoulder to hem	2¾ inches (7 cm)
Width around at underarm	4 inches (10 cm)
Length of sleeve seam	¾ inch (2 cm)

Measurements: Version B

Shoulder to hem	2½ inches (6 cm)
Width around at underarm	4 inches (10 cm)
Length of sleeve seam	½ inch (1.5 cm)

Tension: Version A

9 sts = 1 inch (2.5 cm)

12 rows = 1 inch (2.5 cm)

Tension: Version B

9 sts = 1 inch (2.5 cm)

14 rows = 1 inch (2.5 cm)

Version 1A:
9-inch doll

Instructions

Version A: Using DMC Perle No 5 or Pelicano No. 5 yarn and #1 US (2.25 mm) [13] needles, cast on 20 sts

Version B: Using Sullivan or Milford soft knitting cotton and #0 US (2 mm) [14] needles cast on 20 sts

Front

Versions A & B (Version 1B: Back)

Work three rows in k1, p1 rib

Work 12 rows in st.st

Armhole Shaping

Cast off 1 st at beg of next 2 rows

Version A: Fair Isle decoration

Join in contrasting color (CC)

1st row: *k1 CC, k1 MC, repeat from * to end of row

2nd row: *p1 CC, p1 MC, repeat from * to end of row

3rd row: work as 1st row

Break off CC

4th row: purl

Work 2 rows in st st

Version B: If you want to make a plain sweater, disregard the last 6 rows, and instead work 6 rows in st.st. If you choose to embroider the sweater, this is done on the finished garment, using the graph included on the opposite page.

Versions A & B

Neck Shaping: First Side

7th row: k7, cast off 4 sts, k6, turn

On these 7 sts, knit, dec 1 st at neck edge, in next & following row

Work 2 rows in st.st

Cast off

Neck Shaping: Second Side

Rejoin yarn to neck edge

Next row: purl, dec 1 st at neck edge in next and following row

Work 2 rows in st.st

Cast off

Back: First Side

Versions A & B (Version 1B: Front)

Cast on 20 sts and work 3 rows in k1, p1, rib

Work 8 rows in st.st

Version 2A:
8-inch doll

Version 1B:
8-inch doll

Version A: Back: Second Side

Version 1B: Front: Second Side

9th row: k10, cast on 2 sts, turn

Work 3 rows in st.st

Armhole Shaping

Cast off 1 st at beg of next row

Work 9 rows in st.st

10th row: cast off 4 sts from open edge

Dec 1 st at neck edge in the next 2 rows

Cast off

Back: Second Side

Rejoin yarn to base of opening, cast on 2 sts for underlap

Work 3 rows in st.st, keeping the 2 garter st border

Armhole Shaping

Dec 1 st at end of next row

Work 9 rows in st. st

10th row: cast off 4 sts from back edge

Dec 1 st at neck edge in next 2 rows

Cast off

Short Sleeves (make 2)

Versions A & B

Cast on 16 sts, and work 2 rows in k1, p1, rib

Work 4 rows in st. st

Sleeve Top Shaping

Cast off 1 st at beginning of next 2 rows

Dec 1 st at each end of next and next 3 alternate rows

Cast off remaining sts

To Make Up

Versions A & B: Sew up shoulder seams. Sew sleeves into armholes, sew up sleeve and side seams

Neckband

With right side of work facing you, and using #0 US (2 mm) [14] needles, pick up 28 sts around neck edge

Work 2 rows in k1, p1 rib

Cast off loosely

Version 2B

If you wish to make the design motif shown, mark the center front with a pin and, missing the row below the neckband, follow the graph, with each stitch representing a square, to work the motif in the embroidery color cottons of your choice on the front of the sweater. The design is worked in cross stitch, using three strands of embroidery floss.

Version 2B:
8-inch doll

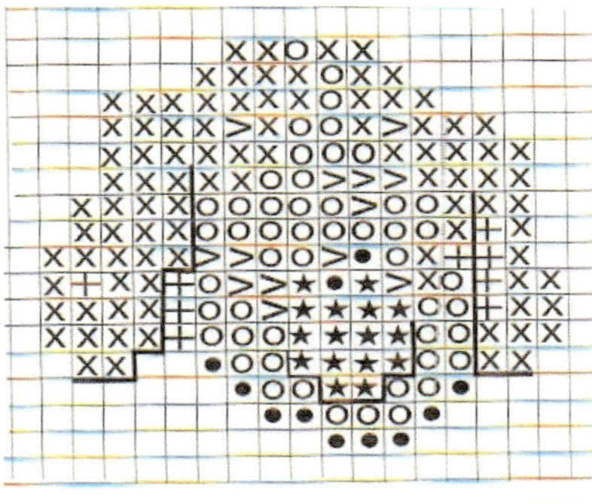

o = white

x = light brown

+ = dark brown

> = black

● = red

★ = pink

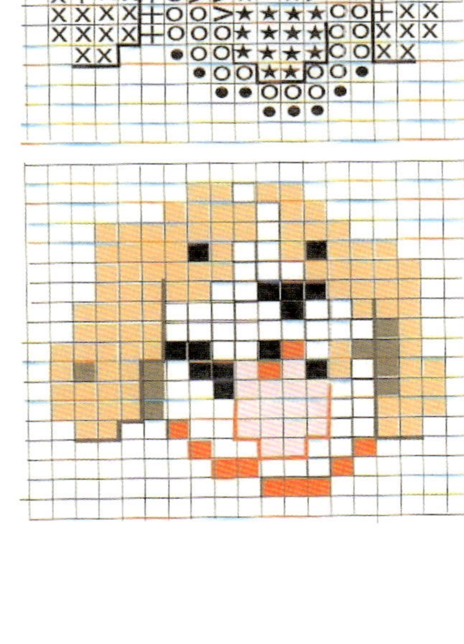

**Knitted Sleeveless or Three-Quarter-Sleeved Blouse

Debbie

8 inches (20 cm) high

This is a versatile item for any doll's wardrobe, whether it be the sleeveless Version A worn by a Betsy McCall from the Tonner Doll Company or the same blouse with three-quarter-length sleeves, Version B, worn by a Ginny doll from the Vogue Doll Company and by Mary Englebreit's Ann Estelle from the Tonner Doll Company.

Version A: Sleeveless Blouse

Materials: Version A
½ ball DMC 20 crochet cotton or equivalent
#0 US (2 mm) [14] knitting needles
3 #4/0 (000 or 5 mm) snaps

Materials: Version B
½ ball DMC Babylo 10 or equivalent
#0 US (2 mm) [14] knitting needles
3 #4/0 (000 or 5 mm) snaps

Measurements: Version A

Length from shoulder to hem	1 7/8 inches (4.5 cm)
Width around at underarm	3½ inches (9 cm)
Width around at hem (open)	4 inches (10 cm)

Measurements: Version B

Length from shoulder to hem	2 1/8 inches (5.5 cm)
Width around at underarm	3½ inches (9 cm)
Width around at hem - open	4 3/8 inches (11 cm)
Length of sleeve seam	5/8 inch (3 cm)

Tension: **Version A**	**Version B**
12 sts = 1 inch (2.5 cm)	12 sts = 1 inch (2.5 cm)
14 rows = 1 inch (2.5 cm)	13 rows = 1 inch (2.5 cm)

Instructions

Work in one piece to armholes
Cast on 45 sts and work 3 rows in ms.st
1st row: knit
2nd row: k2, purl to last 2 sts, k2
Version A: repeat these 2 rows 4 times
Version B: repeat these 2 rows 6 times
Armhole Shaping
Next row: k11, cast off 2 sts, k18, cast off 2 sts, k10

Back: Right Side
Version A: Starting with a purl row, work 8 rows of st.st, keeping the 2 st border on the last 11 sts
Version B: Starting with a purl row, work 10 rows of st.st, keeping the 2 st border on the last 11 sts
Neck Shaping
1st row: cast off 4 sts, purl to end
2nd row: knit
3rd row: p2 tog, purl to end
4th row: knit
Cast off remaining sts

Front

Version A: rejoin yarn to wrong side, work 4 rows in st.st, beginning with a purl row

Version B: rejoin yarn to wrong side, work 6 rows in st.st, beginning with a purl row

Versions A & B:

Next row: p7, p2 tog, p1, p2 tog, p7

Next row: k7, cast off 3, k7

Neck Shaping: First Side

1st row: purl

2nd row: k2 tog, knit to end of row

3rd row: purl

Cast off remaining sts

Neck Shaping: Second Side

1st row: purl

2nd row: knit to last 2 sts, k2 tog

3rd row: purl

Cast off remaining sts

Back: Left Side

Rejoin yarn to remaining sts

1st row: purl to last 2 sts, k2

2nd row: knit

Version A: repeat these 2 rows 2 times, then 1st row 1 time

Version B: repeat these 2 rows 3 times, then 1st row 1 time

Neck Shaping: Versions A & B

Cast off 5 sts at the beg of next row, knit to end

Purl to last 2 st, p2 tog

Knit 1 row

Cast off remaining sts

Collar (make 2)

Version A: cast on 15 sts

Version B: cast on 17 sts

Versions A & B: Work 4 rows of ms.st

Cast off loosely

To Make Up

Version A: **Sew up shoulder seams. Find the center of the neck, and sew each collar in place, starting from the center point**.

Version B: Repeat Version A from ** to **. Sew sleeves in position and sew up sleeve seams.

Sew on snaps to close back opening.

Version B: Three-Quarter-Sleeved Blouse

Version B: Three-Quarter-Sleeved Blouse

*Crocheted Short-Sleeved Cheerleader Sweater or Long-Sleeved Jacket

Denise

8 to 9 inches (20 to 23 cm) high

The short-sleeved version fastens down the back, as modeled by an 8-inch contemporary doll by the Alexander Doll Company, while the long-sleeved version, modeled by a 9-inch doll by the Lawton Doll Company, fastens down the front and can be worn as a blouse or jacket.

Version A: 8-inch doll, short sleeves

Materials: Version A
1 ball DMC Perle No. 8 or equivalent
#8 US (1.25 mm) crochet hook
3 #4/0 (000 or 5 mm) snaps
Stick-on initial designating your favorite team

Materials: Version B
½ ball Babylo 10 or equivalent
4 #4/0 (000 or 5 mm) snaps
4 buttons for front decoration if making a jacket

Measurements	**Version A**	**Version B**
Length from shoulder to hem	2 inches (5 cm)	2 5/8 inches (6.5 cm)
Width around at underarm - fastened	3½ inches (9 cm)	4 inches (10 cm)
Width around at waist - unfastened	4¼ inches (11 cm)	4¾ inches (12 cm)
Length of sleeve seam	3/8 inch (1 cm)	1 5/8 inches (4 cm)

Tension: Version A
10 dc = 1 inch (2.5 cm)
4 rows dc and 3 rows of sc = 1 inch (2.5 cm)

Tension: Version B
9 dc = 1 inch (2.5 cm)
3 rows dc and 3 rows sc = 1 inch (2.5 cm)

Note: when working the sc row, work into the back loop of every dc in the previous row.

Instructions
(work in one piece to armholes)
Make 43 ch, turn and miss 3 ch
1st row: work 1 dc in each ch, 2 ch, turn (40 dc)
2nd row: work 1 sc into the back loop of each dc, 3 ch, turn (40 sc)
Repeat these 2 rows 2 times and then 1st row 1 time
Divide at armholes
8th row: 10 sc, sl st the next 3 dc, 14 sc, sl st the next 3 dc, 10 sc, 3 ch, turn

Back: First Side
9th row: 10 dc, 2 ch, turn
10th row: 10 sc, 3 ch, turn
Repeat last 2 rows 1 time
Neck Shaping
13th row: slip 5 sts, 5 dc, 2 ch, turn
Version A
14th row: 5 sc, 3 ch, turn
15th row: 5 dc
Version B
14th row: 5 sc
Fasten off

Front

Rejoin yarn, miss the 3 slipped sts, and then work 1 dc in each of the next 14 st, 2 ch, turn
2nd row: 14 sc, 3 ch, turn
3rd row: 14 dc, 2 ch, turn
Neck Shaping: First Side
1st row: 5 sc, 3 ch, turn
2nd row: 5 dc
3rd row: 5 sc
Fasten off
Neck Shaping: Second Side
1st row: Miss 4 dc, join yarn, 5 sc, 3 ch, turn
2nd row: 5 dc
3rd row: 5 sc
Fasten off

Back: Second Side

1st row: rejoin yarn, work 10 dc, 2 ch, turn
2nd row: 10 sc, 3 ch, turn
Repeat these 2 rows 1 time
Neck Shaping
5th row: 5 dc, 2 ch, turn
Version A
6th row: 5 sc, 3 ch, turn
7th row: 5 dc
Fasten off
Version B
6th row: 5 sc
Fasten off

Version B: 9-inch doll, long sleeves

Version A: Short Sleeves (make 2)

Make 21 ch, turn, miss 3 ch
1st row: 1 dc in each remaining 18 ch, 2 ch, turn (18 dc)
2nd row: 1 sc in each dc, 3 ch, turn
Sleeve Top Shaping
3rd row: 2 dc tog, 1 dc in each next 14 sc, 2 dc tog, 2 ch, turn (16 sc)
4th row: 2 sc tog, 1 sc in each next 12 st, 2 sc tog, 3 ch, turn (14 sts)
5th row: 2 dc, tog, 1 dc in each next 10 sts, 2 dc tog, 2 ch, turn
6th row: 2 sc tog, 1 sc in each next 8 sts, 2 sc. tog, 3 ch, turn
7th row: 2 dc tog, 1 dc in each next 6 sts, 2 dc, tog, 2 ch, turn
8th row: 2 sc tog, 4 sc, 2 sc tog
Fasten off

Version B: Long Sleeves (make 2)

Make 17 ch, turn, miss 3 ch
1st row: 14 dc, 2 ch, turn
2nd row: 14 sc, 3 ch, turn
Repeat these 2 rows 1 time
5th row: inc in the 1st sc, 12 dc, inc in the last sc, 3 ch, turn
6th row: 16 sc, 2 ch, turn
7th row: inc in the first sc, 14 dc, inc in last sc, 2 ch, turn
8th row: 18 sc, 3 ch, turn
Sleeve Shaping
9th row: 2 dc tog, 1 dc in each of the next 14 sc, 2 dc tog, (16 dc) 2 ch, turn
10th row: 2 sc tog, 12 sc, 2 sc tog (14 sc), 3 ch, turn
11th row: 2 dc tog, 10 dc, 2 dc tog (12 dc), 2 ch, turn
12th row: 2 sc tog, 8 sc, 2 sc tog (10 sc), 3 ch, turn
13th row: 2 dc tog, 6 dc, 2 dc tog (8 dc), 2 ch, turn
14th row: 2 sc tog, 4 sc, 2 sc tog
Fasten off

To Make Up

Sew up shoulder seams. Sew sleeves into armholes, easing to fit if necessary. Sew up sleeve seams. Sew snaps in place to close either back or front opening.
Version A: Decorate with a glue-on initial for your favorite team.
Version B: If jacket opens down the front, decorate with small fancy buttons.

*Crocheted Halter-Neck Blouse

Dixie

8 to 9 inches (20 to 23 cm) high

These fashionable halter-neck blouses are made in Perle No. 5, as seen on a 9-inch 2002 doll by Raikes Collectibles and in Finica No. 10 yarn, as seen on an 8-inch Betsy McCall by the Tonner Doll Company.

Version A:
9-inch doll

Materials: Version A
½ ball DMC Perle No. 5 or equivalent
Small amount of 3 ply rayon silk crochet cotton or equivalent for trim
US No.8 (1.25 mm) crochet hook
3 small buttons (optional)
2 #4/0 (000 or 5 cm) snaps
1 small hook-and-eye

Materials: Version B
1 ball of Finica No. 10 yarn or equivalent
Small amount of DMC No. 10 for trim
US No. 8 (1.25 mm) crochet hook
3 small buttons (optional)
2 #4/0 (000 or 5 mm) snaps
1 small hook & eye

Measurements: Version A

Neck to hem	1¾ inches (4.5 cm)
End halter to hem	3 inches (7.5 cm)
Length from back to waist	1 inch (2.5 cm)
Width around at waist	4 3/8 inches (11 cm)

Measurements: Version B

Neck to hem	1½ inches (4 cm)
End halter to hem	2¾ inches (7 cm)
Length from back to waist	7/8 inch (2.25 cm)
Width around at waist	4 inches (10 cm)

Tension:Version A
9 sc stitches = 1 inch (2.5 cm)
8 rows = 1 inch (2.5 cm)

Tension: Version B
10 sc stitches = 1 inch (2.5 cm)
12 rows = 1 inch (2.5 cm)

Both versions are worked entirely in sc, except for the trim.

Instructions

Starting at waist, make 38 ch, turn, miss 2 ch
1st row: 36 sc, 2 ch, turn
Repeat 1st row 10 times
Fasten off

Front Shaping

1st row: miss 10 sc, join in yarn to next sc, 2 ch, 1 sc in this stitch, 15 sc, 2 ch, turn
2nd row: miss 1 sc, 13 sc, miss 1 sc, 1 sc in next sc, 2 ch, turn
3rd row: 14 sc, 2 ch, turn
Repeat 3rd row 5 times

Neck: First Side and Halter Shaping

9th row: 4 sc, miss 1 sc, 1 sc in next sc, 2 ch, turn
10th row: 5 sc, 2 ch, turn
11th row: repeat 10th row
12th row: miss 1 sc, 4 sc, 2 ch, turn
13th row: 4 sc, 2 ch, turn
14th row: miss 1 sc, 3 sc, 2 ch, turn
15th row: 3 sc, 2 ch, turn
Repeat 15th row 5 times
Fasten off

Neck: Second Side

1st row: miss 2 ch, join in yarn to next st, work 2 ch, 1 sc in this st, miss 1 sc, 4 sc, 2 ch, turn
2nd row: 5 sc, 2 ch, turn
3rd row: repeat 2nd row
4th row: 3 sc, miss 1 sc, 1 sc in last sc, 2 ch, turn
5th row: 4 sc, 2 ch, turn
6th row: repeat 5th row
7th row: 2 sc, miss 1 sc, 1 sc in last sc, 2 ch, turn
8th row: 3 sc, 2 ch, turn
Repeat 8th row 5 times
Fasten off
Versions A & B: Using contrasting yarn, and starting at end of halter, work *1 sc in first st, 1 sc, 3 ch, then join to top of sc (picot)*, repeat from * to * working around neck. End off. Work halter sides and back edge to match.

To Make Up

Fasten back edges with snaps, and join halter ends with a hook and eye. Trim with small buttons or decoration of your choice.

Version B:
8-inch doll

Chapter 5

Jackets and Coats

Whether knitted or crocheted, the jackets and coats in this chapter can be made using a variety of different yarns, which allow them to fit dolls with different-sized chest measurements.

**Knitted Jacket

Eleanor

3½-inch (9-cm) chest

An 8-inch Betsy McCall by the Tonner Doll Company wears the open Version A jacket in a Halloween motif, while an 8-inch doll by the Alexander Doll Company wears the buttoned-up Version B. This jacket can be paired with the "Casey" skirt on page 62 to create the ensemble shown.

Version A: Halloween Motif

Materials: Version A

1 ball DMC No. 20 crochet cotton or equivalent

#0 US (2 mm) [14] knitting needles

Materials: Version B

½ ball DMC Babylo 10 or equivalent in main color (MC)

Small amount DMC Babylo 10 in contrasting color (CC) for trim, cuffs, etc. Additional small ball of contrasting color (CC) if working and weaving the front bands in with the main part of the jacket fronts

#0 US (2 mm) [14] knitting needles

4 #4/0 (000 or 5 mm) snaps

4 fancy buttons for front decoration

Measurements	**Version A**	**Version B**
Shoulder to hem	2 inches (5 cm)	2 inches (5 cm)
Width around at underarm	4 inches (10 cm)	4½ inches (11.5 cm)
Width around at hem	4¾ inches (12 cm)	5½ inches (14 cm)
Length of sleeve seam	1¼ inches (3 cm)	1¾ inches (4.5 cm)

Tension: **Version A**	**Version B**
12 sts = 1 inch (2.5 cm)	11 stitches = 1 inch (2.5 cm)
14 rows = 1 inch (2.5 cm)	14 rows = 1 inch (2.5 cm)

Instructions

Back and Fronts
(knitted in one piece to armholes)

Version A:

**Beginning at the lower edge cast on 51 sts

Work 3 rows in ms.st, k1, p1 rib to last st, k1**

1st row: k1, p1, knit to last 2 sts, p1, k1

2nd row: k1, p1, k1, pl to last 3 sts, k1, p1, k1

Repeat last 2 rows 4 times

Armhole Shaping

Next row: k1, p1, k10, cast off 3 sts, k20, cast off 3 sts, k9, p1, k1

***Front: Left Side

1st row: k1, p1, k1, purl 9

2nd row: k1, p1, k1, k9

Repeat these 2 rows 3 times

Neck Shaping

1st row: cast off 4 sts, purl to end

2nd row: knit

3rd row: p2 tog, purl to end

4th row: knit

Repeat last 2 rows 1 time

Cast off remaining sts***

Version B:

Using CC, work the same as Version A from ** to **

From this point, you will need 2 small balls of contrasting color, one for each jacket edge of 3 ms.st. When changing from CC to MC or MC to CC, weave the stitches on the wrong side of the work (as in multi-color knitting) to give a good joining of the colors.

1st row: using CC, k1, p1, k1, change to MC and knit to the last 3 sts, change to CC, k1, p1, k1

2nd row: using CC, k1, p1, k1, change to MC, purl to last 3 sts, change to CC, k1, p1, k1

Repeat these 2 rows 4 times

Armhole Shaping

Next row: using CC, k1, p1, k1, change to MC, k9, cast off 3 sts, k21, cast off 3 sts, k9, change to CC k1, p1, k1.

Front: Left Side

Continuing using CC for the 3 st border, work from *** to *** as in Version A

Note: if you are unable to weave the CC with the MC, place the 3 st front bands at each end, on a safety pin and work these sts using CC, keeping the main part of the jacket in MC.

Versions A & B: Back

Miss the 3 cast off sts and rejoin yarn to back, beginning with a purl row, p21 sts

2nd row: knit

3rd row: purl

4th row: knit

Repeat last 2 rows 3 times, and 3rd row 1 time

Cast off 6 sts at the beginning of the next 2 rows, work to end of row

Cast off remaining sts

Version A

Front: Right Side

Rejoin yarn to wrong side of remaining 12 sts

1st row: purl to the last 3 sts, k1, p1, k1

2nd row: k1, p1, knit to end of row

Repeat these 2 rows 3 times and 1st row 1 time

Neck Shaping

Cast off 4 sts, knit to end of row

1st row: purl

2nd row: k2 tog, knit to end of row

Repeat these 2 rows 1 time

Cast off remaining sts

Version B

Front: Right Side

Work as Version A, but working the 3 st border in CC

Sleeves (make 2)

Version A: Cast on 15 sts and work 3 rows in ms.st

Version B: using CC, Cast on 15 sts and work 3 rows in ms.st, break off yarn, join in MC

Versions A & B

1st row: knit

2nd row: purl

Repeat these 2 rows 3 times

9th row: inc 1 st at each end of needle

Work 7 rows in st.st

17th row: inc 1 st at each end of needle

Work 3 rows in st.st

Sleeve Top Shaping

Dec 1 st at each end of the next row and following 4 alternate rows

Cast off remaining sts

Note: to sew up sleeve seam easily, roll the sleeve around a pen or pencil.

To Make Up

Gently press. Sew up shoulder seams, sew sleeves into armholes and sew up sleeve seams.

Version A: Decorate with Halloween symbols, if you wish.

Version B: Sew snaps down front, and decorate with fancy buttons.

Version B: High-Fashion Motif

***Crocheted Jacket

Elise

3½-inch (9-cm) chest

A 9-inch limited-edition doll by the Lawton Doll Company wears Version A, a long-sleeved jacket trimmed with white, while a 9-inch doll, made in 2002 by Raikes Collectibles, wears the short-sleeved version with a contrasting collar.

Version A: Long-sleeved jacket

Materials: Version A

1 ball of Pelicano No. 5 or equivalent (this amount is enough to also make a matching pair of slacks)
Small amount of 3 ply silk rayon yarn for trim or equivalent, such as DMC Babylo 10
US #8 (1.25 mm) crochet hook
4 buttons for trim
4 #4/0 (000 or 5 mm) snaps

Materials: Version B

½ ball of Pelicano No. 5 or equivalent in main color (MC)
1 ball of DMC No. 5 in contrasting color for collar (CC)
US #8 (1.25 mm) crochet hook
4 buttons for trim
4 #4/0 (000 or 5 mm) snaps
4 small hooks & eyes to fasten jacket if making for a doll with a slightly larger chest

Measurements: Versions A & B

Length from shoulder to hem	2¾ inches (7 cm)
Width around at underarm fastened	4½ inches (11.5 cm)
Width at underarm (hook & eye fastened)	4¾ inches (12 cm)
Width around at hem	4¾ inches (12 cm)
Length of sleeve seam	Version A: 2 inches (5 cm)
	Version B: ¾ inch (2 cm)

Tension: Versions A & B

8 stitches = 1 inch (2.5 cm)
10 rows = 1 inch (2.5 cm)

Instructions

Versions A & B: Bodice

Make 37 ch, turn, miss 2 ch
1st row: 1 sc in each remaining 35 ch, (35 sc), 2 ch, turn
2nd row: 1 sc in each sc, 2 ch, turn
Repeat 2nd row 4 times
Armhole Shaping & Front: First Side
1st row: 1 sc in each first 9 sc, 2 ch, turn
2nd row: 9 sc, 2 ch, turn
Repeat 2nd row 2 times
Neck Shaping
1st row: sl.st into each of the 1st 4 sc, then 1 sc in each of the next 5 sc, 2 ch, turn
2nd row: 5 sc, 2 ch, turn
Repeat 2nd row 1 time
4th row: miss 1 sc, 4 sc, 2 ch
(Depending on length of doll's torso, you may need to work a 5th row: 2 ch, 4 sc)
Fasten off

Back
Miss the next 2 sc of bodice, join in yarn to next sc, then work 2 ch, 1 sc in this st, work 1 sc in next 12 sc (13 sc), 2 ch, turn
1st row: 13 sc, 2 ch, turn
Repeat 1st row 6 times
8th row: miss 1 sc, 11 sc
Fasten off
Front: Second Side
Miss 2 sc, join in yarn to next sc, then work 2 ch, 2 sc in same st, work 1 sc in each remaining 8 sc (9 sc), 2 ch, turn
1st row: 9 sc, 2 ch, turn
Repeat 1st row 2 times
4th row: 5 sc, 2 ch, turn
Repeat 4th row
6th row: miss 1 sc, 4 sc
Fasten off
(Depending on length of doll's torso, you may need to work an extra row of 4 sc)

Long Sleeves (Version A)

Loosely make 15 ch, miss 2 ch, turn, work 1 sc in each of the remaining 13 ch (13 sc), 2 ch, turn
1st row: 13 sc, 2 ch, turn
Repeat 1st row 3 times
5th row: 2 sc in first sc, 11 sc, 2 sc in last sc (15 sc) 2 ch, turn
6th row: 15 sc, 2 ch, turn
Repeat 6th row 3 times
10th row: 2 sc in first sc, 13 sc, 2 sc in last sc (17 sc) 2 ch, turn
11th row: 17 sc, 2 ch, turn
Repeat 11th row 4 times
Sleeve Top Shaping
**1st row: miss 1 sc, 15 sc, 2 ch, turn
2nd row: miss 1 sc, 13 sc, 2 ch, turn
3rd row: miss 1 sc, 11 sc, 2 ch, turn
4th row: miss 1 sc, 9 sc, 2 ch, turn
5th row: miss 1 sc, 7sc
Fasten off **

Short Sleeves: Version B

Loosely make 17 ch, 2 ch, turn, work 1 sc in each remaining ch (15 sc) 2 ch, turn
1st row: 15 sc, 2 ch, turn
2nd row: 2 sc in first sc, 13 sc, 2 sc, 2 sc in last sc (17 sc) 2 ch, turn
3rd row: 17 sc, 2 ch, turn
Repeat 3rd row 4 times

Sleeve Top Shaping
Work from ** to ** as per long sleeve
Fasten off
Sew up shoulder seams

Collar

Version A: Using MC
Version B: Using CC
With right side of work facing you, work 22 sc
1st row: 22 sc, 2 ch, turn
2nd row: 2 sc in 1st sc, 20 sc, 2 sc in last sc, 2 ch, turn
3rd row: 24 sc, 2 ch, turn
4th row: 2 sc in 1st sc, 22 sc, 2 sc in last sc
Fasten off

Optional Large Pocket: Version A (make 2)

Make 7 ch, turn, miss 2 ch, 1 sc in each remaining ch (5 sc), 2 ch, turn
1st row: 5 sc, 2 ch, turn
Repeat 1st row 3 times
Fasten off

Optional Small Pocket: Version A

Make 5 ch, turn, miss 2 ch, 1 sc, in each remaining 3 ch (3 sc), 2 ch, turn
1st row: 3 sc, 2 ch, turn
Repeat 1st row 1 time
Fasten off

To Make Up

Sew sleeves into armholes, then sew up sleeve seams. Sew collar evenly around neck, leaving 3 scs at each front free to act as a rever.
Version A
Turn back rever, and working on the right side of work, using rayon silk, start at beginning of rever, work 1 sc in each st. Work around rever, then collar, and then to end of 2nd rever. Fasten off.

With right side of main bodice facing you, start at the edge of rever (where you ended off), and work using sc evenly down front, across base of back and then 2nd front edge, to where the rever sc ended. Fasten off.

Work in sc across top of each pocket with silk rayon yarn. Sew pockets in position. Sew snaps in position to close front of jacket. (Note: for a chubbier doll, use hooks & eyes to fasten the front edge.) Decorate with buttons as desired.

Version B: Short-sleeved jacket

*Knitted Poncho

Elizabeth

4- to 4½-inch (10- to 11.5-cm) chest

Ideally suited for both summer, as worn by a 7½-inch Riley by Kish & Company, and for winter, as worn over slacks by a 7½-inch Ginny by the Vogue Doll Company, this poncho is very easy to knit and can be made in an evening.

Version A:
Summer poncho

Materials: Version A

½ spool of white Cameo yarn (MC) (used in punch embroidery) or 2 ply yarn

½ spool of red Cameo (1CC) or 2 ply yarn in a color of your choice

½ spool of green Cameo or 2 ply yarn (2CC) in another color of your choice

#0 US (2 mm) [14] knitting needles

1 #4/0 (000 or 5 mm) snap

Materials: Version B

½ ball of DMC Babylo 10 in blue (MC)

½ ball of DMC Babylo 10 in white (1CC)

½ ball of DMC Babylo 10 in red (2CC)

#0 US (2 mm) [14] knitting needles

1 #4/0 (000 or 5 mm) snap or a small hook & eye

Measurements: Version A

Neck to front point (center front)	2¾ inches (7 cm)
Width across at neck	4 inches (10 cm)
Width around hem	8 inches (20 cm)

Measurements: Version B

Neck to front point (center front)	2 3/8 inches (6 cm)
Width across at neck	3½ inches (9 cm)
Width around hem	7½ inches (19 cm)

Tension: Versions A & B

11 sts = 1 inch (2.5 cm)

14 rows = 1 inch (2.5 cm)

Instructions (make 2)

Note: as you are using three different colors for this poncho, there is no need to cut threads after using each color, just carefully weave them up the side of the garment as you work.

Using 1CC, cast on 43 sts

Work 3 rows in ms.st, change to MC

1st row: k20, sl.1, k2 tog, psso, k20

2nd row: purl, change to 2CC

3rd row: k19, sl.1, k2 tog, psso, k19

4th row: purl, change to MC

5th row: k18, sl.1, k2 tog, psso k18

6th row: purl, change to 1CC

7th row: k17, sl.1, k2 tog, psso, k17

8th row: purl, change to MC

9th row: k16, sl.1, k2 tog, psso, k16

10th row: purl, change to 2CC

11th row: k15, sl.1, k2 tog, psso, k15

12th row: purl, change to MC

13th row: k14, sl.1, k2 tog, psso, k14

14th row: purl, change to 1CC

15th row: k13, sl.1, k2 tog, psso, k13

16th row: purl, change to MC

17th row: k12, sl.1, k2 tog, psso, k12

18th row: purl, change to 2CC

19th row: k11, sl.1, k2 tog, psso, k11

20th row: purl, change to MC

21st row: k10, sl.1, k2 tog, psso, k10

22nd row: purl, change to 1CC

23rd row: k9, sl.1, k2 tog, psso, k9

24th row: purl, change to MC

25th row: k1, *p1, k1, repeat from * to end

26th row: p1, *k1, p1, repeat from * to end

27th row: work as 25th row

Cast off loosely in rib

To Make Up

Matching stripes, sew up one side seam all the way, and the other side seam to within 1½ inches of the neck edge. Fasten at neck with a snap or hook & eye.

Version B:
Winter poncho

*Knitted Coat with Contrasting Border and Collar

Eloise

4½- to 4¾-inch (11.5- to 12-cm) chest

This wonderful coat, with its distinctive border and collar, modeled by a 9-inch wooden doll by Raikes Collectible, can also be worn as a dressing gown by shorter dolls or, by knitting fewer rows, can be made into a jacket, as modeled on an 8-inch 2006 doll by the Alexander Doll Company.

Version A: 9-inch doll wearing coat

Materials: Version A (coat)

2 balls DMC Perle No. 5 or Pelicano No. 5, in main color or equivalent (MC)

2 small balls Sullivan or Milford soft knitting cotton or 4 ply substitute in contrasting color (CC)

#1 US (2.25 mm) [13] knitting needles

1 #4/0 (000 or 5 mm) snap

Small buckel for belt if desired

Materials: Version B (jacket)

1 ball DMC Perle No. 5 or Pelicano No. 5 or equivalent (MC)

2 small balls of DMC No. 5 or Pelicano No. 5 (CC)

#1 US (2.25 mm) [13] knitting needles

1 #4/0 (000 or 5 mm) snap

Small buckel for belt if desired

Measurements	**Version A**	**Version B**
Shoulder to hem	5 7/8 inches (14.5 cm)	3 inches (7.5 cm)
Width around at hem	7¼ inches (18.5 cm)	6¾ inches (17 cm)
Width around at armhole	5¼ inches (13.5 cm)	4½ inches (11.5 cm)
Length of sleeve seam	2 inches (5 cm)	1¾ inches (4.5 cm)
Length of belt	4¾ inches (12 cm)	5 inches (12.5 cm)

Tensions: Version A	**Version B**
10 sts = 1 inch (2.5 cm)	10 ½ sts = 1 inch (2.5 cm)
12 rows = 1 inch (2.5 cm)	14 rows = 1 inch (2.5 cm)

Instructions

Note: both front borders are worked using contrasting yarn along with main color, as a row of main knitting. This is done by weaving the two colors at the inside border edge on each row, similar to knitting a 2-color design. This gives a much better and firmer front band.

Versions A & B (made in one piece to armholes)

Starting at the hem, with contrasting color (CC), cast on 65 sts and work 3 rows in moss st

Change to main color (MC), keeping 3 ms.st border in CC at each end for front borders

Version A: work 20 rows of st.st, starting with a knit row

Version B: work 10 rows in st.st, starting with a knit row, working the main part of jacket using MC, and the first 3 sts at each edge in ms.st using CC

Shaping the Coat/Jacket

1st row: using CC, 3 ms.st, using MC, k14, k2 tog, sl.1, k1, psso, k23, k2 tog, sl.1, k1, psso, k14, using CC, ms.st 3

2nd row: using CC, 3 ms.st, using MC, purl to last 3 sts, using CC, ms.st 3

3rd row: using CC, 3 ms.st, using MC, knit to last 3 sts, using CC, ms.st 3

4th row: work as 2nd row

5th row: using CC, 3 ms.st, using MC, k13, k2 tog, sl 1, k1, psso, k21, k2 tog, sl.1, k1, psso, k13, to last 3 sts, using CC, 3 ms.st

Repeat 2nd to 4th rows

9th row: using CC, 3 ms.st, using MC, k12, k2 tog, sl.1, k1, psso, k19, k2 tog, sl.1, k1, psso, k12, to last 3 sts, using CC, 3 ms.st

Repeat 2nd to 4th rows

13th row: using CC, 3 ms.st, k11, k2 tog, sl 1, k1, psso, k17, k2 tog, sl.1, k1, psso, k11, to last 3 sts, using CC, 3 ms. st

Work 5 rows in st.st, keeping the 3 ms.st in CC border at each end

Armhole Shaping

19th row: using CC, 3 ms.st, with MC, k9, cast off 2 sts, k20, cast off 2 sts, k8, (1 st. is left on needle after casting off) using CC, 3 ms.st

Front: First Side

Work 4 rows in st.st, keeping the 3 ms.st in CC border

Neck Shaping

1st row: using CC, 3 ms.st, using MC, p2 tog, purl to end

2nd row: Using MC, knit to last 5 sts, k2 tog, using CC, 3 ms. st

3rd row: using CC, 3 ms.st, using MC, p2 tog, purl to end

Repeat last 2 rows 1 time

Knit 1 row, keeping 3 ms.st border

Purl 1 row, keeping 3 ms.st border

Cast off MC

***Keeping outside edge of border straight, and continuing in ms.st, inc 1 st at inner edge in next and every following 3rd row, until there are 11 sts on the needle

Work 4 rows in ms.st

Cast off***

Version B: 8-inch doll wearing jacket

Front: Second Side

Rejoin yarn to first 9 sts, starting with a purl row, and keeping the 3 ms. st border, work 5 rows in st.st

1st row: using CC, 3 ms.st, using MC, k2 tog, knit to end

2nd row: using MC, purl to last 5 sts, p2 tog, using CC, 3 ms.st

Repeat last 2 rows 1 time, then 1st row 1 time

6th row: purl

7th row: knit

Cast off MC

Collar Shaping

Work from *** to *** as in instructions for Front: First Side

Back

Rejoin yarn to remaining 21 stitches

Work 11 rows in st.st, starting with a purl row

12th row: cast off 6 sts, knit to end

13th row: cast off 6 sts, purl to end

Cast off remaining sts

Sleeves (make 2)

Versions A & B

Using CC, cast on 15 sts and work 3 rows in ms.st

Change to MC, and work 6 rows in st.st

Inc 1 st at both ends of next row, and following 6th row

Work 3 rows in st.st

Top Sleeve Shaping

Cast off 2 sts at beginning of next 2 rows

Dec 1 st at beginning of next 4 rows (7 sts)

Cast off

Belt

Versions A & B

Using CC, cast on 40 sts

Using MC, knit 1 row, purl 1 row

Using CC, knit 1 row

Cast off

To Make Up

Sew up shoulder seams. Sew up seam at back of collar. Place pin at middle of back neck on coat and pin at join of collar. Ease remaining edging along right side, pinning at intervals and sew in place. Repeat for left side. Sew up sleeves and sew into position. Sew snap in place at waist, then sew buttons on front for decoration. If desired, sew small buckle on belt.

Emily

4-inch (10-cm) chest

These quickly made coats are attractive winter outfits for your doll. Version A, with matching knitted two-tone hat, is worn by 7½-inch Riley by Kish & Company, while an 8-inch doll by the Alexander Doll Company wears Version B, with a simple crocheted white hat with a turned-up brim. (Directions for both hats can be found on page 106.)

Version A:
7½-inch doll

Materials: Versions A & B

Ball of Sullivan or Milford soft knitting cotton (equal to 4 ply) or equivalent

Small amount of contrasting color (CC) Sullivan or Milford soft knitting cotton or equivalent

#0 US (2 mm) [14] knitting needles

6 #4/0 (000 or 5 mm) snaps

6 small buttons

Measurements: Version A

Shoulder to hem	4 inches (10 cm)
Waist to hem	2 inches (5 cm)
Width around at underarm (closed)	4½ inches (11.5 cm)
Width around at underarm (open)	5½ inches (14 cm)
Width around hem	6 inches (15 cm)
Length of sleeve seam (including cuff)	2 inches (5 cm)

Measurements: Version B

Shoulder to hem	4 inches (10 cm)
Waist to hem	2 inches (5 cm)
Width around at underarm (closed)	5 inches (12.5 cm)
Width around at underarm (open)	6 inches (15 cm)
Width around hem	7 inches (17.5 cm)
Length of sleeve seam (including cuff)	2¼ inches (5.5 cm)

Tension: Versions A & B

10 sts = 1 inch (2.5 cm)

4 patterns (16 rows) = 1 inch (2.5 cm)

Instructions

Skirt
(knitted sideways)

Starting at the front edge, cast on 20 sts
Pattern
1st row: knit
2nd row: purl
3rd row: knit
4th row: knit
Continue in pattern until 92 rows have been worked from beginning.
Cast off

Bodice: Back

Starting at the waist, cast on 22 sts, and work 24 rows in pattern
Cast off

Bodice Front: Left Side

Starting at the waist, cast on 12 sts, and work 24 rows in pattern
Cast off

Bodice Front: Right Side

Starting at the waist, cast on 18 sts, and work 24 rows in pattern
Cast off

Sleeves (make 2)
(worked sideways)

Cast on 18 sts, work 22 rows in pattern
Cast off

Cuffs

Using contrasting color (CC), pick up and knit 13 sts along one side edge of sleeve
Knit 6 rows in garter st
Cast off loosely

Collar

Using main color (MC), cast on 35 sts, change to contrasting color (CC)
Knit 11 rows in garter st
Cast off

To Make Up

Sew up 5 sts from armhole edge to form shoulder seams. Open out bodice and place a large pin in the middle of the back neck. Also place pins 5 sts in from both front edges of neck. Fold collar and place a large pin at halfway point. Matching center pins, sew collar between the two pins at neck edge of dress.

At the end of the 4th pattern from bottom of each piece of bodice, place a pin. Sew top of each sleeve between pins on appropriate side. Sew up sleeve and side seams.

Place a pin in the middle of the finished bodice hem, and also in the middle of one side edge of skirt. With right sides of both bodice and skirt outwards, pin front bodice to one end of skirt, and other side bodice to other end. Match center pins. Ease remaining skirt to suit bodice, and sew the two pieces together.

Turn up cuffs on sleeves, if needed.

Place finished coat on doll, crossing over as shown in photo. Sew snaps on right front edge to close coat; then sew snaps on the left front to close the underneath section of the overlap. Sew the buttons in twos evenly down the front of the coat to create a double-breasted effect.

Version B:
8-inch doll

Chapter 6

Slacks and Shorts

These slacks and shorts are ideal accompaniments to the sweaters, blouses and jackets in the earlier chapters.

Faith

4- to 4½-inch (10- to 11.5-cm) waist

Dolls of the same height may have legs of different lengths. Both versions of this pattern fit 9-inch dolls, but Version A, worn by a 2002 Raikes Collectibles doll, is slightly longer than Version B, which fits a 9-inch doll by the Lawton Doll Company.

Version A: Longer Length (5 inches from waist)

Materials: Versions A & B

1 ball of Pelican Perle No. 5 or equivalent such as DMC No. 5

US #8 (1.25 mm) crochet hook

Short length of thin elastic

Measurements: Version A

Length from waist to hem	5 inches (12.5 cm)
Length from waist to crotch	2 inches (5 cm)
Length of inside leg	3 inches (7.5 cm)
Width around at waist	4¼ inches (11 cm)

Measurements: Version B

Length from waist to hem	4½ inches (11.5 cm)
Length from waist to crotch	2 inches (5 cm)
Length of inside leg	2½ inches (6 cm)
Width around at waist	4¼ inches (11 cm)

Tension: Versions A & B

7 stitches = 1 inch (2.5 cm)

10 rows = 1 inch (2.5 cm)

Instructions (make 2)
(both versions worked sideways)

Leg (make 2)

Version A
Make 36 ch, turn, miss 2 ch, 1 sc in each remaining ch (34 sc), 2 ch, turn
1st row: 34 sc, 2 ch, turn
Repeat 1st row 3 times
**5th row: 28 sc, sl.st into next st,1 ch, turn
6th row: 28 sc, 2 ch, turn
7th row: 34 sc, 2 ch, turn
Repeat 7th row 3 times **
Repeat 5th to 10th rows 3 times
Fasten off

Version B
Make 32 ch, miss 2 ch, 1 sc in each remaining ch, (30 sc), 2 ch, turn
1st row: 30 sc, 2 ch, turn
Repeat 1st row 3 times
**5th row: 25 sc, sl.st, into next st, 1 ch, turn
6th row: 25 sc, 2 ch, turn
7th row: 30 sc, 2 ch, turn
Repeat 7th row 3 times**
Repeat from ** to ** 3 times
Fasten off

To Make Up

Starting from the waist (short width), sew the first 12 sts of two side seams together to form the center front. Then sew the 1st 12 sts of the other two side seams together to form the center back. Sew up leg seams, starting at one hem and ending at the other.

Waistband

Join in yarn to center back, work 1 sc in each next 3 ends of rows, *miss 1 end of row, work 1 sc into each next 3 row ends*, repeat from * to * to end of row, 2 ch, turn
Next row: 1 sc in each sc
Fasten off
Thread thin elastic through waist, or fasten waistband with a snap.

Version B: Shorter Length (4½ inches from waist)

*Knitted Slacks with Fancy Cuffs

Fay

4-inch (10-cm) waist

These slacks or knee pants, depending on the height of the doll, may be part of a summer ensemble, or could even be paired with a matching or contrasting top to form pajamas. If you would like to make long shorts, turn up the cuffs of the slacks.

Version A:
7½-inch doll

Materials: Versions A & B
1 ball of DMC Babylo 10 in main color (white) or equivalent (MC)
Small amount of DMC Babylo 10 in contrasting color or equivalent (1CC)
#0 US (2 mm) [14] knitting needles
Short length of thin elastic
Version B: Small amount of DMC Babylo 10 in another contrasting color (2CC)

Measurements: Version A

Waist to crotch	2 inches (5 cm)
Length of outer leg, cuff down	3¾ inches (9.5 cm)
Length of outer leg with cuff	3 inches (7.5 cm)
Length of inner leg, cuff down	2 inches (5 cm)
Length of inner leg with cuff	1½ inches (4 cm)
Width around waist	4½ inches (11.5 cm)

Measurements: Version B

Waist to crotch	2 inches (5 cm)
Length of outer leg	3¾ inches (9.5 cm)
Length of inner leg	2 inches (5 cm)
Width around waist	4½ inches (11.5 cm)

Tension: Versions A & B
12 sts = 1 inch (2.5 cm)
14 rows = 1 inch (2.5 cm)

Instructions

Leg (make 2)

Version A

***Using MC and starting at waist, cast on 27 sts

1st row: *k1, p1, repeat from * to last st, k1

2nd row: *p1, k1, repeat from * to last st, p1

Repeat 1st row

4th row: knit

Beginning with a purl row, work 17 rows in st st

Inc 1st at both ends of the next 3 rows

Purl 1 row

Cast on 2 sts at beginning of next 2 rows

Work 7 rows in st.st

Dec 1 st at each end of next 2 rows

Work 3 rows in st.st

Repeat these 4 rows 3 times ***

Colored Band

With contrasting color (1CC), work 11 rows in garter st

Break off yarn

Version B

Work the same as Version A from *** to ***

Colored Band

1st & 2nd rows: using MC, knit

3rd & 4th rows: using 1CC, knit

5th & 6th rows: using 2CC, knit

7th & 8th rows: using 1CC, knit

9th & 10th rows: using MC, knit

Cast off

To Make Up

With wrong sides together, sew up front and back center seams. Sew up inside leg seams. If necessary, thread thin elastic through waist to fit doll's waist. Turn up color band at base of legs in Version A if you want "pedal pushers" or capris.

Version B:
8-inch doll

*Knitted Long Shorts

Felicity

3½- to 4-inch (9- to 10-cm) waist

An 8-inch Betsy McCall by Tonner Doll Company models these long shorts. The pattern for her sleeveless blouse, "Debbie," can be found on page 76.

Materials

1 ball DMC Babylo 10 yarn or equivalent in main color (MC)
Small amount of DMC Babylo 10 yarn in contrasting color (CC)
#0 US (2 mm) [14] knitting needles
Short length of thin elastic

Measurements

Waist to crotch	1¾ inches (4.5 cm)
Length of outside leg seam (contrasting color down)	3¼ inches (8.5 cm)
Length of inside leg seam (contrasting color down)	1½ inches (4 cm)
Width around at waist	4 inches (10 cm)

Tension

12 sts = 1 inch (2.5 cm)
14 rows = 1 inch (2.5 cm)

Instructions

Leg (make 2)

Cast on 27 sts
Work 4 rows in k1, p1 rib
Work 6 rows in st.st
Next row: inc 1 st at each end of row
Work 7 rows in st.st
Next row: inc 1 st at each end of row (29 sts)
Purl 1 row
Repeat last 2 rows 1 time
Cast on 2 sts at beg of next 2 rows
Work 2 rows
Next row: dec 1 st at each end of row
Work 3 rows in st.st
Repeat last 4 rows 2 times
Change to contrasting color (CC) and work 7 rows in ms.st
Cast off

To Make Up

With wrong sides of work facing you, sew up back and front seams. Sew up inside leg seams. The contrasting color section can be left down to create long knee pants, or turned up to make cuffed long shorts.

Fleur

4½-inch (11.5-cm) waist

These versatile shorts, modeled by a 9-inch vintage Patsy look-alike, can be teamed with a variety of tops for many different looks. She wears "Debbie," on page 76, with stick-on decorations.

Materials

1 ball of DMC Perle No. 5 or Pelicano No. 5 equivalent
#0 US (2 mm) [14] knitting needles
Short length of thin elastic
Stick-on decoration, if desired

Measurements

Length from waist to hem	2 inches (5 cm)
Length from waist to crotch	1½ inches (4 cm)
Width around waist	5 inches (12.5 cm)

Tension

11 sts = 1 inch (2.5 cm)
14 rows = 1 inch (2.5 cm)

Instructions

Right Leg

Cast on 32 sts
Work 3 rows in k1, p1 rib
Next row: k16, turn, sl.1, purl to end of row
Work 8 rows in st.st
Leg Shaping
Inc 1 st. at beg of next 4 rows
Cast on 2 sts at beg of next 2 rows
Work 4 rows in st.st
Cast off using a purl st

Left Leg

Cast on 32 sts
Work 3 rows in k1, p1 rib
Next row: p16, turn, sl.1, knit to end of row
Work 9 rows in st. st
Leg Shaping
Inc 1 st at beg of next 4 rows
Cast on 2 sts at beg of next 2 rows
Work 4 rows in st.st
Cast off using a purl st

To Make Up

Sew up front and back seams. Sew crotch seam. Thread fine elastic through the rib sts at waist. Decorate with a stick-on emblem, if you wish.

Flora

3½-inch (9-cm) waist

These shorts are modeled by a 9-inch doll by Raikes Collectibles, which wears a pair with contrasting hem trim, while the plainer Version B is worn by an 8-inch Betsy McCall by the Tonner Doll Company.

Version A:
9-inch doll

Materials: Versions A & B

½ ball DMC Babylo 10 or equivalent (Note: sometimes denier (thickness) of yarn can be slightly finer due to color of yarn.)

#8 US (1.25 mm) crochet hook

Short length of thin elastic

Small amount of contrasting color yarn for trim for Version A, if desired

Measurements: Version A

Length of waist to hem	2¼ inches (5.5 cm)
Length of waist to crotch	2 inches (5 cm)
Length of inside leg seam	½ inch (1.5 cm)
Width around waist	3¼ inches (9.5 cm)

Measurements: Version B

Length of waist to hem	2 inches (5 cm)
Length of waist to crotch	1¾ inches (4.5 cm)
Length of inside leg seam	3/8 inch (1 cm)
Width around waist	4 inches (10 cm)

Tension: Version A	**Version B**
8 stitches = 1 inch (2.5 cm)	9 stitches = 1 inch (2.5 cm)
10 rows = 1 inch (2.5 cm)	11 rows = 1 inch (2.5 cm)

Instructions (make 2)
(worked sideways)
Make 18 ch, turn, miss 2 ch, 1 sc in each remaining ch (16 sc), 2 ch, turn
1st row: 16 sc, 2 ch, turn
Repeat 1st row 3 times
**5th row: 12 sc, sl.st into next st, 1 ch, turn
6th row: 12 sc, 2 ch, turn
7th row: 16 sc, 2 ch, turn
Repeat 7th row 3 times**
Repeat the 6 rows from ** to ** 3 times

To Make Up
Sew up front and back seams by sewing together the 1st 12 sc from the waist. Sew up leg seam from hem to hem.

Waistband
Join in yarn to center back, work 1 sc into each of the next 3 row ends, *miss 1 row end, 1 sc in each of the next 3 row ends*, repeat from * to * to end of row. Thread thin elastic through waistband to fit doll's waist, or fasten waistband with a snap.
Version A: using contrasting yarn, work 1 sc in each row end around each leg hem.

Version B: 8-inch doll

Chapter 7

Hats

These hats have been made to complement some of the outfits in this book but, of course, by changing the colors and/or yarns, you may create your own versions to wear with any outfit of your choosing.

*Knitted Hat with Contrasting Brim

Gail

This hat is the finishing touch for the "Emily" coat on page 92. Version A, with the turned-up brim, is worn by a 2006 8-inch doll by the Alexander Doll Company. Version B, with a contrasting brim, is worn by 7½-inch Riley by Kish & Company. The same hat with the brim turned down at the front is worn by a 9-inch doll by the Lawton Doll Company.

Version A

Materials: Versions A & B

Small ball of Milford No. 8 knitting cotton, DMC Petra or equivalent (MC)

Small amount of contrasting color yarn, Milford No. 8, DMC Petra, or equivalent for brim (CC)

#1 US (2.25 mm) [13] knitting needles

Measurements: Version A

Length from crown to edge of brim	1¼ inches (3 cm)
Circumference around at brim	5 inches (13 cm)

Measurements: Version B

Length from crown to edge of brim	1¾ inches (4.5 cm)
Circumference around at brim	5 inches (13 cm)

Tension: Versions A & B

9 sts = 1 inch (2.5 cm)

10 rows = 1 inch (2.5 cm)

Instructions

Brim

Using MC (Version A) or CC (Version B), contrasting color (CC), cast on 42 sts

Version A

Knit 5 rows

Version B

Knit 10 rows

Change to main color (MC) and knit 7 rows (8 to 9 rows if you want the hat to have a deeper base before working the crown)

Crown

1st row: *k5, k2 tog, repeat from * to end of row

2nd & all alternate rows: knit

3rd row: *k4, k2 tog, repeat from * to end of row

5th row: *k3, k2 tog, repeat from * to end of row

7th row: *k2, k2 tog, repeat from * to end of row

8th row: knit

Break off yarn, leaving at least 12 inches (30 cm)

To Make Up

Thread yarn onto needle, and then thread the needle through the remaining sts on needle. Pull up all sts into a tight circle, and end off securely. Sew up side seam and brim. Version B: Turn up half of contrasting color, leaving portion at front down, to create a different effect.

Version B

Version B

**Crocheted Hat with Turned-up Brim

Georgia

The hat with the turned-up brim, worn in Version A by a 7½-inch Riley, and in Version B in another color by an 8-inch doll by the Alexander Doll Company, will fit any doll with a 5-inch head circumference.

Version A

Materials: Version A

Small amount of DMC or Coats No. 20 crochet cotton or equivalent

#8 US (1.25 mm) crochet hook

Length of matching ribbon for band

Materials: Version B

Small amount of DMC Babylo 10 or equivalent

#8 US (1.25 mm) crochet hook

Length of matching or contrasting ribbon for band

Measurements: Version A	
Crown to base	1¼ inches (3 cm)
Length of brim	¼ inch (.5 cm)
Width around at hatband	5 1/8 inches (13 cm)
Width around/brim turned up	6½ inches (16 cm)
Measurements: Version B	
Crown to base	1¼ inches (3 cm)
Length of brim	¼ inch (.5 cm)
Width around at hatband	6 inches (15 cm)
Width around/brim turned up	7½ inches (19 cm)

Tension: Versions A & B

12 dc = 1 inch (2.5 cm)

Instructions

Make 4 ch and join into a circle

1st round: 2 ch, then work 8 sc into circle

2nd round: 2ch, *1 sc in 1st sc, 2 sc in next sc, repeat from * to end of round, join to top of 2 ch

3rd round: 2 ch, * 1 sc into each of the next 2 sc, 2 sc into the next sc, repeat from * to end of round, join to top of 2 ch

4th round: 3 ch, 1 dc into next dc, *2 dc into next dc, 1 dc in each of the next 2 dc, repeat from * to end of row, join to top of beginning 3 ch

5th round: 3 ch, 1 dc into each of the next 2 dc, *2 dc into next dc, 1 dc in each of the next 3 dc, repeat from * to end of round, join to top of beginning 3 ch

6th round: 3 ch, 1 dc into each of the next 3 dc, *2 dc into next dc, 1 dc in each of the next 4 dc, repeat from * to end of round, join to top of beginning 3 ch

7th round: 2 ch, 1 sc in each dc, join to top of beginning 3 ch

8th round: 2 ch, 1 sc in each sc, join to top of beginning 2 ch

9th round: 3 ch, 1 dc in next sc, *2 dc in next sc, 1 dc in next sc, repeat from * to end of round, join to top of beginning 3 ch

To Make Up

Sew in ends, spray with starch and either turn up brim, or iron it flat. To make an even firmer hat, brush fabric stiffener on the inside, form shape, and leave aside to dry. Using fabric glue, glue ribbon on top of 7th and 8th round for hatband.

Version B

**Crocheted Hat with Wide Brim

Germaine

This wide-brimmed hat complements many outfits. It is worn in Version A by a circa-1990s doll made in China and in Version B by an 8-inch doll by the Alexander Doll Company. It is also a nice finishing touch for the "Beverley" dress on page 47.

Version A

Materials: Version A

1 ball DMC No. 20 or Coats No. 20 crochet cotton

#8 US (1.25 mm) crochet hook

12 inches (30 cm) of thin ribbon for decoration

Materials: Version B

½ ball DMC Babylo 10 or equivalent

#8 US (1.25) crochet hook

12 inches (30 cm) of thin ribbon for decoration

Measurements: Version A

Length from top of crown to base of crown	1 inch (2.5 cm)
Length of brim	½ inch (1.5 cm)
Width around at base of crown	5 inches (12.5 cm)
Width around brim	8½ inches (21.5 cm)

Measurements: Version B

Length from top of crown to base of crown	1¼ inches (3.5 cm)
Length of brim	¾ inch (2 cm)
Width around at base of crown	6 inches (15 cm)
Width around brim	9½ inches (24 cm)

Tension: Versions A & B

12 dc = 1 inch (2.5 cm)

5 rows dcs = 1 inch (2.5 cm)

Instructions

Work 5 ch and join into a ring, 2 ch

1st round: 8 sc into ring

2nd round: 2 ch, 1 sc into 1st sc *, 1 ch, 1 sc into next, repeat from * to end, join to top of 2 ch

3rd round: 2 ch, *2 sc into each 1 ch space, repeat from * to end of round, sl.st into top of 2 ch

4th round: 3 ch, 1 dc into first sc, *2 dc into next sc, 1 dc into next sc, repeat from * to end of round, join with a sl.st into top of 3 ch

5th round: 3 ch, 1 dc in each of the next 2 dc, *2 dc in next dc, 1 dc in of the next 2 dc, repeat from * to end of round, join with a sl.st into top of 3 ch

6th round: 3 ch, 1 dc in each of the next 3 dc, *2 dc in next, 1 dc in each of the next 3 dc, repeat from * to end of round, join with a sl.st into top of 3 ch

7th round: 3 ch, 1 dc in each of the next 4 dc, *2 dc in next, 1 dc in each of the next 4 dc, repeat from * to end of round, join with a sl.st into top of 3 ch

8th round: 3 ch, 1 dc in each dc, join to top of 3 ch

9th round: 3 ch, 1 dc in 1st dc, *2 dc in next dc, 1 dc in next dc repeat from * to end of round, join to top of 3 ch

10th round: repeat 9th round

Fasten off

To Make Up

Version A: Thread ribbon through dc row at base of crown, and tie in a bow at back.

Version B: Glue ribbon evenly around base of crown, crossing it over at middle of back; glue in position, leaving ends to hang free, at the length you desire, over brim.

Version B

**Crocheted Beaded Headband

Glenda

This accessory is ideal for pairing with ballerina outfits or party frocks.

Materials

Small amount of No. 20 crochet cotton
#7 US (1.5 mm) crochet hook
40 small beads in matching color
Length of ¼ inch matching ribbon

Measurements

Length of band	4½ inches (11.5 cm)
Length of beaded area	2 inches (5 cm)

Instructions

Thread 40 beads onto thread
Make 42 ch, turn
1st row: miss 2 ch, 1 sc in each ch to end (40 ch), 2 ch, turn
2nd row: 1 sc in each of the first 10 sc, slide 1 bead along thread, then *work 1 sc into next st (trapping a bead), repeat from * 19 times, then 1 sc in each of the next 10 sc
Fasten off
Join yarn to other side of basic chain
Repeat 2nd row 1 time
Fasten off

To Finish

Attach a length of ribbon at both ends of band so you can tie band at back of the head, under the doll's hair.

Gloria

Worn here by an 8-inch doll by the Alexander Doll Company, this elegant little hat is quickly made.

Materials
1 ball DMC Perle No. 5 or Pelicano Perle No. 5 or equivalent
#8 US (1.25 mm) crochet hook
Length of matching ribbon for decoration, if you wish

Measurements

Width across crown	1 5/8 inches (4 cm)
Length of side from crown to brim	½ inch (1.5 cm)
Width around brim	6 inches (15 cm)

Tension
9 dc = 1 inch (2.5 cm)

Instructions

Make 5 ch and join into a ring
1st round: 8 sc into the ring, join to top of first sc
2nd round: 2 ch, *1 sc in first sc, 2 sc in next sc, repeat from * to end of round, join to top of 2 ch
3rd round: 2 ch *1 sc in each of the next 2 sc, 2 sc in next sc, repeat from * to end of round, join to top of 2 ch
4th round: 2 ch, *1 sc in each of the next 3 sc, 2 sc in next sc, repeat from * to end of round, join to top of 2 ch
5th round: 2 ch, *1 sc in each of the next 4 sc, 2 sc in next sc, repeat from * to end of round, join to top of 2 ch
6th round: 3 ch, *1 dc in next sc, 2 dc in next sc, repeat from * to end of round, join to top of 3 ch
7th round: 3 ch, *1 dc in each of the next 2 dc, 2 dc in next dc, repeat from * to end of round, join to top of 3 ch
8th round: 2 ch, 1 sc in each dc, join to top of 2 ch
9th & 10th rounds: repeat 8th round
Fasten off

To Make Up

Darn in ends. If you can find a pill bottle that has a lid with the right circumference, cover with plastic wrap. If not, cut a circle of cardboard 1 5/8 inches in diameter, cover with plastic wrap. Paint the inside of the hat with a brush using fabric softener, and place crown over lid, or cardboard inside top of crown, pull into shape. Leave aside to dry. Remove lid or cardboard when thoroughly dry. Decorate as you wish.

Chapter 8

Sleepwear

Because every doll needs a bedtime wardrobe, patterns are given for dressing gowns/housecoats, nightgowns and pajamas for every season.

**Knitted Dressing Gown/Housecoat

Hannah

7½ to 8 inches (19 to 20 cm) high

This shaped gown is modeled by 7½-inch Riley in Version A and by an 8-inch doll by the Alexander Doll Company in Version B, but it can also be made as a coat for 9-inch dolls.

Version A: 7½-inch doll

Materials: Version A
DMC Perle No. 5 or Pelicano No. 5
#1 US (2.25 mm) [13] knitting needles
2 #4/0 (000 or 5 mm) snaps
3 buttons for decoration

Materials: Version B
1 ball of Sullivan or Milford soft knitting cotton (equal to 4 ply) or equivalent
Small amount of Sullivan or Milford soft knitting cotton in a contrasting color (CC) for collar, cuffs and belt
#0 US (2 mm) [14] knitting needles
3 #4/0 (000 or 5 mm) snaps
2 buttons for decoration

Measurements	**Version A**	**Version B**
Length from shoulder to hem	5½ inches (14 cm)	5 inches (12.5 cm)
Width around at underarm (unclosed)	5 inches (12.5 cm)	5 inches (12.5 cm)
Width around at hem	7¼ inches (18.5 cm)	7 inches (18 cm)
Length of sleeve seam (cuff turned up)	1½ inches (4 cm)	
Length of sleeve seam (cuff down)	1¾ inches (4.5 cm)	1¾ inches (4 cm)
Length of belt	11 inches (28 cm)	11 inches (28 cm)

Tension: Version A	**Version B**
9 sts = 1 inch (2.5 cm)	10 sts = 1 inch (2.5 cm)
10 rows = 1 inch (2.5 cm)	13 rows = 1 inch (2.5 cm)

Instructions

Version A
Starting at the hem, using Pelicano No. 5 or DMC Perle No. 5, and #1 US (2.25 mm) [13] needles, cast on 65 sts

Version B
Starting at the hem, using Sullivan or Milford soft knitting cotton and #0 US (2 mm) (14) needles, cast on 65 sts

Versions A & B
1st - 3rd row: *k1, p1 repeat from * to last st, k1
4th row: k1, p1, k1, knit to last 3 sts, k1, p1, k1
5th row: k1, p1, k1, purl to last 3 sts, k1, p1, k1
Repeat 4th & 5th rows 9 times
(Note: if you want a longer gown for a taller doll, add more rows here. Check tension to see how many you will require to get the length desired: 10 rows = 1 inch.)
24th row: k1, p1, k15, k2 tog, sl.1, k1, psso, k23, k2 tog, sl.1, k1, psso, k15, k1, p1 (61 sts)
25th - 27th rows: continue in st.st, keeping the 3 st ms.st border at each end of work
28th row: k1, p1, k14, k2 tog, sl.1, psso, k21, k2 tog, sl.1, k1, psso, k14, p1, k1 (57 sts)
29th - 31st rows: repeat 25th - 27th rows
32nd row: k1, p1, k13, k2 tog, sl.1, psso, k19, k2 tog, sl.1, k1, psso, k13, p1, k1 (53 sts)

33rd - 35th rows: repeat 25th - 27th rows
36th row: k1, p1, k12, k2 tog, sl.1, psso, k17, k2 tog, sl.1, k1, psso, k12, p1, k1 (49 st)
Work 15 rows in st.st, starting with a purl row, keeping the ms.st borders as before
Divide for armholes
Next row: k1, p1, k1, k9, cast off 2 sts, k20, cast off 2 sts, k8, k1, p1, k1

Front: First Side
1st row: k1, p1, k1, p9
2nd row: k10, p1, k1
Repeat these 2 rows 2 times
Neck Shaping
1st row: cast off 5 sts, purl to end
2nd row: knit to last 2 sts, k2 tog
3rd row: purl
4th row: knit
5th row: knit
Cast off remaining sts

Back
Rejoin yarn to middle 21 stitches to make the back
Work 11 rows in st.st
12th row: cast off 6 sts, knit to end
13th row: cast off 6 sts, purl to end
Cast off remaining sts

Version B: 8-inch doll

Front: Second Side
Rejoin yarn to last 12 sts
Keeping the 3 sts, ms.st border, work 7 rows in st.st
8th row: cast off 5 sts at beg of row, knit to end
9th row: purl to last 2 sts, p2 tog
10th row: knit
11th row: purl
12th row: knit
Cast off

Sleeves (make 2)
Version A
Cast on 15 sts, work 3 rows in ms.st
Version B
Using contrasting yarn (CC), cast on 15 sts and work 4 rows of ms.st, end off and change to main color (MC)
Versions A & B
Beginning with a knit row, work 6 rows in st.st
7th row: inc at both ends of row
Work 5 rows in st.st
13th row: repeat 7th row
Work 3 rows in st.st
Sleeve Top Shaping
Cast off 2 sts at beginning of next 2 rows, then dec 1 st at both ends of next and every alternate row until 9 sts remain
Cast off

Collar
Version A
Cast on 31 sts and work 5 rows in ms.st
Version B
Using CC, cast on 31 sts and work 5 rows in ms.st
Versions A & B
6th row: work in ms.st until 8 sts remain, turn
7th row: sl.1, work in ms.st until 8 sts remain, turn
8th row: sl.1, work in ms.st to end
Cast off

Belt
Cast on 91 sts, work 3 rows in ms.st
Cast off

To Make Up
Sew up shoulder seams. Pin cast-off edge of collar to neck of gown, leaving the 3 st border free. Sew in position. Sew sleeve seams, and sew into armholes. Sew snaps down front to below waist to close. Decorate with buttons down front; tie belt at front.

***Crocheted Dressing Gown/Housecoat

Harriet

7½ to 9 inches (19 to 23 cm) high

Two 9-inch dolls from different eras, a 2002 wooden doll by Raikes Collectibles and a 1960s vinyl English Patch doll, wear this crocheted dressing gown. The pattern can be easily shortened to fit a smaller doll, such as a 7½-inch Ginny by the Vogue Doll Company, which models Version B.

Version A: 9-inch doll

Materials: Version A

1 ball of Pelicano No. 5 or DMC Perle No. 5 or equivalent (MC)

Small amount of Pelicano No. 5 or DMC Perle No. 5 or equivalent in contrast color (CC)

#7 US (1.5 mm) crochet hook

3 #4/0 (000 or 5 mm) snaps

Materials: Version B

1 ball of Pelicano No. 5 or DMC Perle No. 5 or equivalent (MC)

Small ball of angora or mohair yarn in contrasting color (CC) of choice

#7 US (1.5 mm) crochet hook

3 #4/0 (000 or 5 mm) snaps

Buttons for decoration

Measurements:	**Version A**	**Version B**
Length from shoulder to hem	6¾ inches (17 cm)	5½ inches (14 cm)
Length from waist to hem	5 inches (12.5 cm)	3¾ inches (9.5 cm)
Width around at underarm (closed)	4½ inches (11.5 cm)	4½ inches (11.5 cm)
Width around at hem	7½ inches (19 cm)	8½ inches (21.5 cm)
Length of sleeve seam	1¾ inches (4.5 cm)	1¾ inches (4.5 cm)

Tension: Versions A & B

7 dc = 1 inch (2.5 cm)

7 rows of skirt pattern = 1 inch (2.5 cm)

NOTE: the skirt of the dressing gown can be made to fit a shorter doll by working less sc/dc when making the skirt, but keeping the same number of shaping sts at the waist end; specific instructions follow.

Instructions

Skirt

(worked sideways)

Note: instructions for Version A are given first, followed by instructions for Version B in parentheses.

Work 39 ch, turn, miss 3 ch (Version B: make 29 ch, turn, miss 3 ch)
1st row: 1 dc in each ch, 2 ch, turn (Version B: 1 dc in each ch, 2 ch, turn)
2nd row: 6 sc, 30 dc, 2 ch, turn (Version B: 6 sc, 20 dc, 2 ch, turn)
3rd row: 36 sc, 2 ch, turn (Version B: 26 sc, 2 ch, turn)
4th row: 36 sc, 2 ch, turn (Version B: 26 sc, 2 ch, turn)
5th row: 36 sc, 2 ch, turn (Version B: 26 sc, 2 ch, turn)
Versions A & B
Repeat last 4 rows 10 times
Fasten off (right front edge)

Bodice: Versions A & B

(worked in one piece to armholes)

Rejoin yarn to right front edge and work 34 sc evenly along short side of skirt, ending with a 2 ch, turn
1st row: 34 sc, 2 ch, turn
Repeat 1st row 5 times
Armhole Shaping
Front: First Side
7th row: 9 sc, 2 ch, turn
Work 6 rows of 9 sc, 2 ch, turn
14th row: 5 sc, 2 ch, turn
15th row: miss 1 sc, 4 sc, 2 ch, turn
16th row: 4 sc
Fasten off
Back
Miss 2 sc, rejoin yarn and work 12 sc, 2 ch for back, turn
Work 8 rows of 12 sc, 2 ch, turn
Neck Shaping: First Side
1st row: 4 sc, 2 ch, turn
2nd row: 4 sc
Fasten off
Neck Shaping: Second Side
1st row: miss 5 sc, rejoin yarn, 4 sc, 2 ch, turn
2nd row: 4 sc
Fasten off
Front: Second Side
Miss 2 sc, rejoin yarn, 1 sc in each of the remaining 9 sc, 2 ch, turn
Work 6 rows of 9 sc, 2 ch, turn
Neck Shaping
1st row: sl.st 4 sts, 5 sc, 2 ch, turn
2nd row: miss 1 sc, 4 sc, 2 ch, turn
3rd row: 4 sc
Fasten off

Sleeves (make 2)

(worked sideways)

Version A
Make 17 ch, turn
1st row: miss 2 ch, 2 sc in each of the remaining 15 ch (15 sc)
2nd row: 14 sc, 2 sc in last st, 2 ch, turn

Version A:
9-inch doll

Version B:
7½-inch doll

3rd row: 16 sc, 2 ch, turn
4th row: sl.st 3 sts, 12 sc, 2 sc in last st, 2 ch, turn
5th row: 17 sc, 2 ch, turn
6th row: sl.st 3sts, 13 sc, 2 sc in last st, 2 ch, turn
7th row: 18 sc, 2 ch, turn
8th row: sl.st 3 sts, 14 sc, 2 sc in last st, 2 ch, turn
9th row: 19 sc, 2 ch, turn
10th row: sl.st 3 sts, 14 sc, miss 1 sc, 1 sc, 2 ch, turn
11th row: 18 sc, 2 ch, turn
12th row: sl.st 3 sts, 13 sc, miss 1 sc, 1 sc, 2 ch, turn
13th row: 17 sc, 2 ch, turn
14th row: sl.st 3 sts, 12 sc, miss 1 sc, 1 sc, 2 ch, turn
15th row: 16 sc, 1 ch, turn
16th row: 14 sc, miss 1 sc, 1 sc, 1 ch, turn
17th row: 15 sc
Fasten off
Version B
Make 15 ch, turn
1st row: miss 2 ch, 2 sc in each remaining ch (13 ch)
2nd row: 12sc, 2sc in last sts, 2 ch, turn
3rd row: 14 sc, 2 ch, turn
4th row: sl.st 3sts, 10sc, 2sc in last st., 2 ch, turn
5th row: 15 sc, 2 ch, turn
6th row: sl.st 3 sts., 11 sc, 2sc in last st, 2 ch, turn
7th row: 16 sc, 2 ch, turn
8th row: sl.st 3 sts, 12 sc, 2 sc in last st, 2 ch, turn
9th row:17 sc, 2 ch, turn
Repeat last row 4 times
14th row: sl.st. 3 sts 12 sc, miss 1 sc, 1 sc, 2 ch, turn
Work 15th to 17th row as Version A
Fasten off

Collar

Version A
Sew up shoulder seams. With right side of work facing you, miss the first 4 sc on right front, join yarn and work 32 sc evenly along front neck, back neck and other side front neck, 1 ch, turn.
Work 5 rows of sc on these 32 sts.
Fasten off
Version B
Using angora or mohair yarn, work as Version A.

To Make Up

Version A
Sew sleeves in position; sew up sleeve seams. Using a contrasting color (CC), start at lower edge of right side front, work 1 sc in each sc of skirt and, at end of each row of bodice, across front neck, and around collar, (working 3 sts in each corner st), and along front edge of left side, and down 3 rows. Fasten off. Sew snaps on bodice to close. If you wish, you may crochet a chain of CC as a belt.
Version B
Sew sleeves in position; sew up sleeve seams. Using angora or mohair yarn, work as per Version A instructions, and work 1 sc in each row end of bodice, each st of skirt, working from left front edge, down left front side, around hem and up right front, and work 3 sc in each corner. Using MC, crochet a length of chain for belt, then miss 2 ch, and work 1 sc in each ch, fasten off. Sew snaps down front to close, and decorate with fancy buttons.

Hayley

7½ to 9 inches (19 to 23 cm) high

Every doll needs a winter nightdress; a long version (A) is worn by a 9-inch doll by artist Heidi Pluszczok and by 9-inch Lightly Lily by the Lawton Doll Company. A shorter version (B) is worn by a 7½-inch Ginny by the Vogue Doll Company.

Materials: Version A

1 ball of Sullivan or Milford soft 4 ply knitting cotton or equivalent

#0 US (2 mm) [14] knitting needles

1 #4/0 (000 or 5 mm) snap

Materials: Version B

1 ball Pelicano Perle No. 5 or DMC Perle No. 5 in main color (MC)

Small amount of DMC Perle No. 5 in contrasting color (CC)

#0 US (2 mm) [14] knitting needles

1 #4/0 (000 or 5 mm) snap

Measurements: Version A

Shoulder to hem	6½ inches (16.5 cm)
Bottom of yoke to hem	5¼ inches (13.5 cm)
Width around at underarm	5 inches (12.5 cm)
Width around at hem	9½ inches (24 cm)
Length of sleeve seam	2 inches (5 cm)

Measurements: Version B

Shoulder to hem	5½ inches (14 cm)
Bottom of yoke to hem	4¼ inches (11 cm)
Width around at underarm	4½ inches (11.5 cm)
Width around at hem	10 inches (25.5 cm)
Length of sleeve seam	1¾ inches (4.5 cm)

Tension: Version A	**Version B**
11 sts = 1 inch (2.5 cm)	12 sts = 1 inch (2.5 cm)
2 patterns = 1 inch (2.5 cm)	2 patterns = 1½ inches (4 cm)

Version A: 9-inch doll

Instructions

Pattern

1st row: k5, *p1, k7, repeat from * to last 5 sts, p1, k4

2nd row: p3, *k1, p1, k1, p5, repeat from * to last 7 sts, k1, p1, k1, p4

3rd row: k3, *p1, k3, repeat from * to last 3 sts, p1, k2

4th row: p1, *k1, p5, k1, p1, repeat from * to last st, k1

5th row: k1, *p1, k7, repeat from * to last st, p1

6th row: p1, *k1, p5, k1, p1, repeat from * to last st, k1

7th row: k3, *p1, k3, repeat from * to last 3 sts, p1, k2

8th row: p3, *k1, p1, k1, p5, repeat from * to last 7 sts, k1, p1, k1, p4

Version A:
9-inch doll

Skirt

(worked in one piece to armholes)

Starting at the hem, cast on 97 sts

Work 3 rows in garter st, increasing 1 st at end of 3rd row

Version A: Work the pattern rows 9 times, then repeat the first 4 rows of pattern again

Version B: work the pattern 7 times

Versions A & B

Dec row: (k2 tog 5 times), *sl 1, k2 tog, psso* repeat from * to * 26 times, then (k2 tog, 5 times) (36 sts)

Starting with a purl st, work 2 rows in ms.st (seed st)

Back Bodice: First Side

Armhole Shaping

Work 9 sts in ms.st, turn

Work 9 rows of ms.st on these 9 sts

Neck Shaping

Cast off 5 sts, work to end

Work 3 rows in ms.st on the remaining 4 sts

Cast off

Front Bodice

Rejoin yarn to remaining sts, k2 tog, then *p1, k2 repeat from * 4 times, p1, k2 tog, turn

Work 8 rows of ms.st on these 15 sts

Neck Shaping: First Side

Keeping continuity of ms.st, work 6 sts, cast off 3 sts, work to end

1st row: work 4 sts, k2 tog

2nd row: k2 tog, work to end of row

Work 1 row

Cast off

Neck Shaping: Second Side

Rejoin yarn to remaining side of neck

1st row: work 2 tog, work 4 sts

2nd row: work to last 2 sts, work 2 tog

Work 1 row

Cast off

Back Bodice: Second Side

Rejoin yarn to remaining 10 sts

Work 9 rows in ms.st

Cast off 5 sts, work in ms.st to end

Work 3 rows in ms.st

Cast off

Version A: Long Sleeves (make 2)

Cast on 15 sts and work 4 rows in ms.st, increasing 1 st at each end of last row (17 sts)

**1st row: k4, p1, k7, p1, k4

2nd row: p3, k1, p1, k1, p5, k1, p1, k1, p3

3rd row: k2, p1, k3, p1, k3, p1, k3, p1, k2

4th row: p1, k1, p5, k1, p1, k1, p5, k1, p1

5th row: inc, k7, p1, k7, inc

6th row: k1, p1, k1, p5, k1, p1, k1, p5, k1, p1, k1

7th row: *k3, p1, repeat from * to last 3 st, k3

8th row: p4, k1, p1, k1, p5, k1, p1, k1, p4

9th row: k5, p1, k7, p1, k5

10th row: p4, k1, p1, k1, p5, k1, p1, k1, p4

11th row: inc, k2, *p1, k3 repeat to last 3 sts, k2, inc

12th row: p1, k1, p1, k1, p5, k1, p1, k1, p5, k1, p1, k1, p1

13th row: k2, p1, k7, p1, k7, p1, k2

14th row: repeat 12th row

15th row: *p1, k3, repeat to last st, p1

16th row: p5, k1, p1, k1, p5, k1, p1, k1, p5 **

17th row: inc, k5, p1, k7, p1, k5, inc

18th row: k1, p5, k1, p1, k1, p5, k1, p1, k1, p5, k1

19th row: k1 *p1, k3 repeat to last 2 sts, p1, k1

20th row: p2, k1, p1, k1, p5, k1, p1, k1, p5, k1, p1, k1, p2

21st row: k3, p1, k7, p1, k7, p1, k3

22nd row: repeat 20th row

23rd row: repeat 19th row

24th row: repeat 18th row

Sleeve Top Shaping

Keeping pattern as now set, cast off 3 sts at beginning of next 2 rows

Dec 1 st at both ends of next row, and every alternate row until 11 sts remain

Cast off

Version B: Long Sleeves (make 2)

Using contrasting color (CC), cast on 15 sts and work the 4 rows in ms.st and inc at each end of last row (17 sts), change to MC

Work as Version A from ** to ** (rows 1 - 16)

Sleeve Top Shaping

Cast off 2 sts at beginning of next 2 rows

Dec 1 st at both ends of next row and every following alternate row, until 9 sts remain

Cast off

Collar (make 2)

Version A

Cast on 21 sts

Work 7 rows in ms.st

Cast off

Version B

Using CC, work as Version A

To Make Up

Press with a warm iron. Sew up shoulder seams. Sew sleeves in position, easing to fit armhole. Sew up sleeve seams. Place pin at center front of neckline. Sew each collar from this point to within 3 sts of back edge of neck.

Version B: 7½-inch doll

*Knitted Winter PJs

Heather

7½ to 8 inches (19 to 20 cm) high

These charming winter pajamas are worn by a 7½-inch Riley by Kish & Company, who models Version A, and an 8-inch contemporary doll by the Alexander Doll Company, who models Version B. Of course, the jacket pattern can be used alone to create a jacket of any sort, and the pattern for the bottoms can also be used to create slacks.

Version A:
7½-inch doll

Materials: Versions A & B

1 ball Milford or Sullivan 4 ply knitting cotton in main color (MC)

Small ball of Milford or Sullivan 4 ply knitting cotton in contrasting color (CC)

#0 US (2 mm) [14] knitting needles

3 #4/0 (000 or 5 mm) snaps

Buttons for decoration

Embroidery thread for decoration

Small length of thin elastic for waist of pants, if needed

Measurements

Jacket: Versions A & B

Length from shoulder to hem	2½ inches (6.5 cm)
Width around hem	5½ inches (14 cm)
Width around chest (closed)	5 inches (12.5 cm)
Length of sleeve seam	1¾ inches (4.5 cm)

Pants	**Version A**	**Version B**
Width around at waist	4 inches (10 cm)	4 inches (10 cm)
Length from waist to cuff	3¾ inches (9.5 cm)	4 inches (10 cm)
Length from waist to crutch	1½ inches (4 cm)	1 7/8 inches (4.5 cm)
Length of inside leg	2¼ inches (6 cm)	2 3/8 inches (6 cm)

Tension: Version A	**Version B**
10 sts = 1 inch (2.5 cm)	10 sts = 1 inch (2.5 cm)
14 rows = 1 inch (2.5 cm)	14 rows = 1 inch (2.5 cm)

Instructions

Pajama Jacket

(worked in one piece to armholes)

Beginning at the lower edge, cast on 49 sts and knit 3 rows in garter st

1st row: k2, p1, k43, p1, k2

2nd row: k3, p43, k3

Version A: repeat 1st & 2nd rows 6 times

Version B: repeat 1st & 2nd rows 7 times

Armhole Shaping

k2, p1, k11, cast off 2 sts, k16, cast off 2 sts, k10, p1, k2

Front: First Side

On last 14 sts, and keeping the 3 st border as set, purl 1 row

1st row: k2 tog at armhole edge work to end of row

2nd row: purl
Repeat these 2 rows 1 time
5th row: knit
6th row: purl
7th row: 1 row
Neck Shaping
Cast off 4 sts, purl to end
1st row: k2 tog at neck edge
2nd row: purl
Repeat these 2 rows 1 time
Cast off
Back
Rejoin yarn to base of 17 sts for the back
Work 12 rows in st.st
Neck Shaping
Cast off 5 sts at beginning of next 2 rows
Cast off remaining sts
Front: Second Side
Rejoin yarn to the remaining 14 sts, and keeping the 3 st border as set
1st row: purl
2nd row: k2 tog at armhole edge

How To Make a Lazy Daisy Stitch

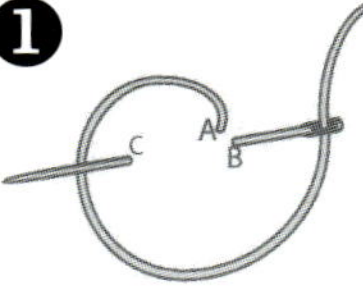

1. Bring the needle through at A. Insert the needle at B and bring it up at C, making sure the thread is underneath the needle.

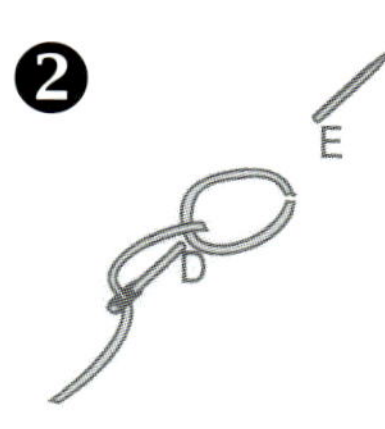

2. Draw the needle through the fabric, place it over the looped thread, and insert it at D, then bring the needle up at E ready to make the next petal.

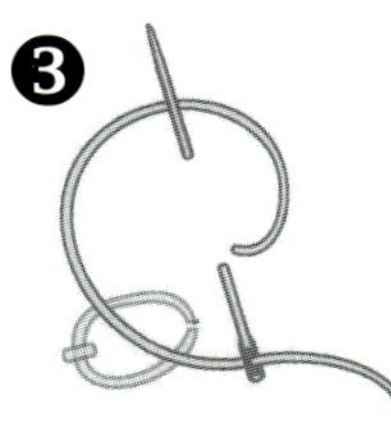

3. Any number of petal stitches may be worked to form a flower; in this case 4 petals were used.

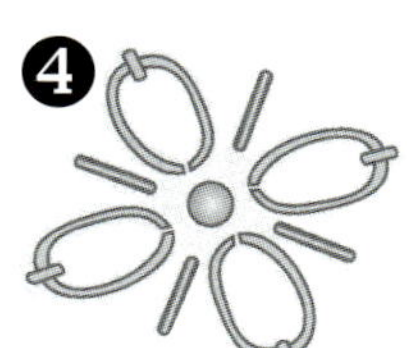

4. With contrasting or main color work a straight stitch between each petal as shown.

3rd row: purl
Repeat last 2 rows 1 time
6th row: knit
7th row: purl
Neck Shaping
8th row: cast off 4 sts, knit to end
9th row: purl
10th row: knit to last 2 sts, k2 tog
11th row: purl
Repeat last 2 rows 1 time
Cast off

Sleeves

Version A
Cast on 14 sts and knit 2 rows in garter sts
Version B
Using contrasting color (CC), cast on 14 sts and knit 2 rows in garter st, break off CC, join in MC and continue as follows
Versions A & B
Knit 4 rows in st.st
Working in st.st, inc 1 st at both ends of next row
Version A: work 13 rows in st. st
Version B: work 11 rows in st. st
Versions A & B
Dec 1 st at each end of next, and following alternate rows until 6 sts remain
Cast off

Collar

Version A
Using main color (MC), cast on 30 sts
Change to CC, knit 6 rows
Cast off loosely
Version B
Using CC, cast on 30 sts
Knit 6 rows
Cast off

To Make Up

Sew up shoulder seams. Pin collar in place, leaving garter st edge free to allow for crossover. Sew collar in place. Sew up sleeves and sew in place. Sew three snaps down front, and buttons to decorate.
Version A: Embroider a flower at each front corner of jacket. Using a contrasting color of embroidery yarn, work 4 lazy daisy

stitches (see diagram on page 125), then work 1 small straight st. in same color between each daisy st. Using MC, finish with a French knot in middle of the 4 daisy sts.

Version B: Using each st to represent a square, embroider a small emblem such as a teddy-bear head on each side of front. Refer to the chart below.

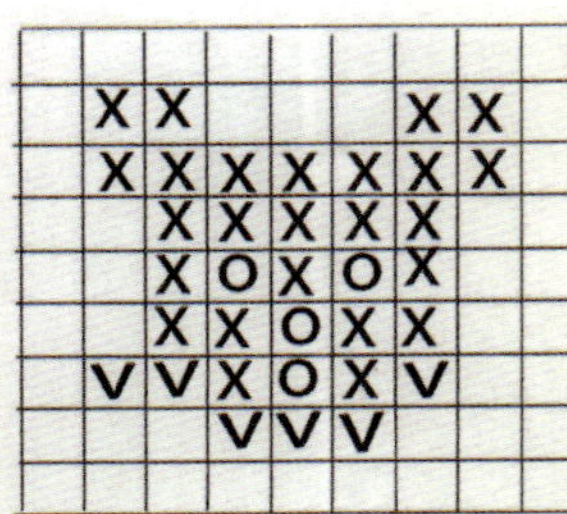

x = gold or yellow embroidery yarn (use the full 6 strands)
o = brown embroidery yarn for nose and eyes.
v = embroidery yarn for neck decoration of your choice

Pants

Beginning at waist edge, cast on 20 sts
Work 3 rows in k1, p1 rib
Version A: work 4 rows in st.st
Version B: work 6 rows in st.st
Versions A & B: inc 1 st at both ends of next row, and following 4th row 2 times (26 sts)
Version A: work 3 rows in st. st
Version B: work 5 rows in st. st
Versions A & B: tie a colored thread at each end of row to denote where leg shaping begins
Leg Shaping
Cast off 1 st at beginning of next 2 rows
Work 8 rows in st.st
9th row: dec 1 st at both ends of row
Work 9 rows in st. st
19th row: dec 1 st at both ends of row
Work 9 rows in st. st.
29th row: dec 1 st at both ends of row
(Note: leg may be lengthened or shortened here by knitting more or less rows, depending on length of doll's legs.)
Work 6 rows of sts.st
Version A: change to CC, purl 2 rows
Knit 1 row
Cast off
Version B: using MC, purl 2 rows
Knit 1 row
Cast off

To Make Up

With wrong sides facing you, sew up front and back seams. Then sew up leg seams. Thread thin elastic through waist, if needed.

Version B:
8-inch doll

Helen

7½ inches (19 cm) high

Version A of these crocheted short summer pajamas is worn by Riley by Kish & Company, while Version B is worn by Ginny by the Vogue Doll Company. Both dolls are 7½ inches high.

Version A: 7½-inch doll

Materials: Version A
1 ball No. 8 crochet cotton in main color (MC)
Small amount of No. 8 crochet cotton in contrasting color (CC)
#8 US (1.25 mm) crochet hook
2 #4/0 (000 or 5 mm) snaps
Short length of thin elastic

Materials: Version B
1 ball No. 8 Perle crochet cotton (cheaper variety) in main color (MC)
Small amount of No. 8 crochet cotton in contrasting color (CC)
#7 US (1.5 mm) crochet hook
2 #4/0 (00 or 5 mm) snaps
Short length of thin elastic
½ yard of thin ribbon for trim

Tension: Version A
10 dc = 1 inch (2.5 cm)
4 rows sc, plus 3 rows of dc = 1 inch (2.5 cm)

Tension: Version B
11 dc = 1 inch (2.5 cm)
4 rows sc, plus 3 rows of dc = 1 inch (2.5 cm)

Measurements	**Version A**	**Version B**
Top		
Shoulder to hem	2½ inches (6.5 cm)	3 inches (7.5 cm)
Depth of yoke	½ inch (1.5 cm)	5/8 inch (1.5 cm)
Width around at under arm	4 inches (10 cm)	4½ inches (11.5 cm)
Width around at hem	7 inches (18 cm)	12 inches (30.5 cm)
Pants		
Length from waist to crotch	1¾ inches (4.5 cm)	2 3/8 inches (6 cm)
Length of side seam (minus trim)	1½ inches (4 cm)	1½ inches (4 cm)
Width around at waist	4 inches (10 cm)	4¼ inches (11 cm)

Abbreviation Note
Shell: work 5 dc into one st

Instructions

Top

Yoke: Versions A & B

Starting at the neck edge, using contrasting color (CC), make 32 ch fairly loosely, turn, miss 2 ch

1st row: 1 sc in each of the ch to the end of the row, 2 ch, turn (30 sc)

2nd row: *1 sc in each of the first 2 sc, 2 sc in the next sc, rep from * to end of row, 2 ch, turn (40 sc)

3rd row: *1 sc in each of the first 3 sc, 2 sc in the next sc, rep from * to end of row, 2 ch, turn (50 sc)

4th row: *1 sc in each of the first 4 sc, 2 sc in the next sc, rep from * to end of row, 2 ch, turn

5th row: *1 sc in each of the first 5 sc, 2 sc in the next sc, rep from * to end of row, 2 ch, turn (70 sc)

6th row: working through the front loop of each stitch only, work as follows, 1 sc in first sc, *3 ch, miss 1 sc, 1 sc in next, repeat from * to end of row

Fasten off

Version B

7th row: 3 ch, turn, 1 sc in each of the 3 ch loops, 3 ch (This gives a lovely fine lace-like edge to the yoke.)

Fasten off

Bodice & Skirt

Join in main color (MC)

Armhole Shaping

Version B:
7½-inch doll

1st row: Working in the back loop only of the sts in the yoke, work 1 sc in each of the next 11 sc, 6 ch (loosely), miss 14 sc, 1 sc in each of the next 20 sc, 6 ch (loosely), miss 14 sc, 1 sc in each of the last 11 sc, 2 ch, turn

2nd row: 1 sc in each sc, plus 1 sc in each of the 6 ch of the armholes, 3 ch, turn (54 sc)

3rd row: 1 dc in each sc, 3 ch, turn

4th row: 1 dc in each of the first 5 dc, * 1 dc, 1 ch, 1 dc into next dc, 1 dc in each of the next 6 dc, repeat to end of row, 3 ch, turn

5th row: 1 dc in each of the first 5 dc, miss 1 dc, * 2 dc, 1 ch, 2dc into 1 ch space between dc in previous row; miss 1 dc, 1 dc in each of the next 6 dc, repeat to last 5 sts, 5 dc, 3 ch, turn

6th row: 1 dc in each of the first 5 dc, miss 2 dc, *2 dc, 1 ch, 2 dc into 1 ch space between dc in previous row, miss 2 dc, 1 dc in each of the next 6 dc, repeat to last 5 sts, 5 dc, 3 ch, turn

7th row: 3 dc, *1 dc, 1 ch, 1 dc into space between the 3rd and 4th dc of previous row, 1 dc in each of the next 3 dc, miss next 2 dc, 5dc (shell) into 1 ch space, miss next 2 dc, 3 dc, repeat from * to end of row, 3 ch, turn

8th row: 2 dc, miss 1 dc, 5 dc (shell) into 1 ch space, *miss 2 dc, 1 dc in next dc, miss 3 dc, 5 dc in center dc of shell, miss 3 dc, 1 dc in next dc, miss 2 dc, 5 dc in 1 ch space, repeat to end of row, 3 ch, turn

9th row: 2 dc, *5 dc in center dc of shell, 1 dc on single dc, repeat from * to end of row, working 1 dc in each of last 2 dc, 3 ch, turn

10th row: 2 dc, * 5 dc in center dc of shell, 3 dc into top of the single dc, repeat to the end of row, finishing with 2 dc, 3 ch, turn

11th row: 2 dc, * 5 dc in center dc of shell, 3 dc in center dc of 3 dc in previous row, repeat from * to end of row, finishing with 1 dc, 3 ch, turn

12th row: 2 dc, *5 dc in center dc of shell, 5 dc in center of 3 dc, repeat from * finishing with 2 dc, 3 ch, turn

13th row: 2 dc, *5 dc in center dc of shell, repeat from * along row, finishing with 2 dc

Fasten off

To Make Up

Sew up the back seam for the first four rows from the hem. Close the back opening with a snap at the back neck edge.

Pants (make 2)

Using MC, make 22 ch, turn, miss 2 ch

1st row: 1 sc in each chain (20 sc), 3 ch, turn

2nd row: 1 dc in each st (20 dc) 2 ch, turn

Repeat these 2 rows 1 time

5th, 7th & 9th rows: inc 1 sc at each end of row, 3 ch, turn

6th, 8th & 10th rows: 1 dc in each sc, 1 ch, turn

11th row: sl.st into the first 5 sts, 1 sc in the next 18 sts, 2 ch, turn

12th row: sl.st into the first 5 sts, 2 ch, 8 dc, 2 ch, turn

13th row: miss 1 st, 5 sc, miss 1 st, 1 sc, 3 ch, turn

14th row: miss 1 st, 3 dc, miss 1 st, 1 dc, 3 ch, turn

15th row: 4 dc

Fasten off

To Make Up and Finish Off

Sew the two pieces together at the bottom 4 dc edge.Work edging as follows: using CC, with the right side of work facing you, work around the leg opening.

1st row: *1 sc in first st, 2 sc in next, repeat around leg opening, 3 ch, turn

2nd row: *1 dc in each sc, repeat to end of row, 2 ch, turn

3rd row: *1 sc in each dc, repeat to end of row, 2 ch, turn

4th row: 1 sc in 1st st, *3 ch, miss 1 sc, 1 sc in next sc, repeat from * to end of row

Sew up side seams. If necessary, thread fine elastic through waist row.

**Crocheted Nightie

Hilary

6½ to 7 inches (16 to 18 cm) high

This quick-to-make nightdress can be made in the sleeveless Version A, as seen on a 7-inch Amanda Jane, or with long sleeves (Version B), seen on a 6½-inch Hitty by Raikes Collectibles.

Version A: 7-inch doll

Materials: Versions A & B

½ spool of Cameo acrylic yarn (used for punch embroidery) or the equivalent (2 ply yarn) in main color (MC)
Small amount of Finca No. 8 crochet cotton, or equivalent (2 ply yarn) in contrasting color (CC)
#7 US (1.5 mm) crochet hook
2 #4/0 (000 or 5 mm) snaps

Measurements: Versions A & B

Length from shoulder to hem	4¾ inches (12 cm)
Width around at underarm	3½ inches (9 cm)
Width around at hem	4 inches (10 cm)
Length of optional sleeve seam	1¾ inches (4.5 cm)

Tension: Versions A & B

9 dc = 1 inch (2.5 cm)
5 rows of dc = 1 inch (2.5 cm)

Instructions

(worked in one piece to armholes)
39 chain, turn, miss 3 ch
1st row: 1 dc in each chain (36 dc), 3 ch, turn
2nd row: 1 dc in each dc
3rd row: join in contrasting color (CC), 2 ch, 1 sc in each dc, 2 ch, turn
4th row: 1 sc in each sc
5th row: using main color (MC), 3 ch, 1 dc in each sc, 3 ch, turn
6th row: 1 dc in each dc
7th & 8th rows: using CC, work as 3rd & 4th rows
Break off CC
9th row: using MC, 3 ch, 1 dc in each sc, 3 ch, turn
10th row: 1 dc in each dc, 3 ch, turn
Repeat last row 8 times
19th row: 4 dc, dec by working the next 2 dc tog, *4 dc, dec repeat from * to end, (30 dc), 3 ch, turn
20th row: 1 dc in each dc, 2 ch, turn
21st row: 1 sc in each dc, 2 ch, turn

Back: First Side

Yoke and Armhole Shaping

1st row: 1 sc in the first 7 sc, 2 ch, turn

Repeat this row 5 times

Neck Shaping

1st row: sl st, 3 sc, 4 sc, 2 ch, turn

2nd row: 1 sc in each sc, 2 ch, turn

Repeat 2nd row 2 times

Fasten off

Front Yoke

1st row: miss the next two sc on skirt, 1 sc in each of the next 12 sc, 2 ch, turn

2nd row: 1 sc in each sc (12 sc), 2 ch, turn

Repeat 2nd row 4 times

Neck Shaping: First Side

1st row: 1 sc in each of the first 4 sc, 2 ch, turn

*2nd row: 1 sc in each of the 4 sc, 2 ch, turn

Repeat 2nd row 2 times

Fasten off*

Neck Shaping: Second Side

Miss 3 sc, rejoin yarn, and work 1 sc in each of the next 4 sc, 2 ch, turn

Version B: 6½-inch doll

Repeat from * to * as worked on first side of neck shaping

Back: Second Side

Miss 2 sc on skirt, 1 sc in each of the remaining 7 sc, 2 ch, turn

1st row: 1 sc in each sc, 2 ch, turn

Repeat this row 4 times

Neck Shaping

1st row: 1 sc in the first 4 sc, 2 ch, turn

2nd row: 1 sc in each sc

Repeat 2nd row 2 times

Fasten off

Yoke Frill

Make 42 ch, turn, miss 2 ch, 1 sc in each ch (40 sc), 3 ch, turn

1st row: 2 dc in first sc, miss 1 sc, *1 sc in next sc, miss 1 sc, 5 dc in next, miss 1 sc, repeat from * to last sts, miss 1 sc, 3 dc in last sc

Fasten off

Version B: Long Sleeves (make 2)

Using CC, work 14 ch, miss 2 ch, turn

1st row: 1 sc in each ch (12 sc), 2 ch, turn

2nd row: 1 sc in each sc

Fasten off CC

3rd row: join in MC, 3 ch, 2 dc in first sc, 1 sc in each of the next 10 sc, 2 dc in last st (14 dc), 3 ch, turn

4th row: 1 dc in each dc, 3 ch, turn

Repeat 4th row 2 times

7th row: 2 dc in 1st dc, 1 dc in each dc to last st, 2 dc in last st, 3 ch, turn (16 dc)

8th row: 1 dc in each dc, 3 ch, turn

Repeat 8th row 2 times

Sleeve Top Shaping

1st row: miss the 1st dc, 1 dc in each of the next 12 dc, miss 1 dc, 1 dc in last st, 3 ch, turn

2nd row: miss the 1st dc, 1 dc in each of the next 10 dc, miss 1 dc, 1 dc in last st, 3 ch, turn

3rd row: miss the 1st dc, 1 dc in each of the next 8 dc, miss 1 dc, 1 dc in last st, 3 ch, turn

4th row: miss the 1st dc, 1 dc in each of the next 6 dc, miss 1 dc, 1 dc in last st

Fasten off

Version B: Neck Edging

Sew up shoulder seams. Join in CC at back edge of neck, and work 2 ch, *1 sc, 3 ch, repeat around neck to other back edge, 1 sc. Fasten off.

To Make Up

Sew up shoulder seams. Fold frill in half, and place center shell at center front of yoke. Pin rest of frill equally across front and over shoulders to back (3 shells should go across front yoke). Sew frill in place. Sew up back seam for 3 inches from hem. Sew on snaps to close back opening. Version B: Sew sleeves in armholes, and sew up sleeve seam. (You will find it easier to sew sleeve seam if you roll sleeve section around a pencil.)

Chapter 9

Sportswear

Owners often like to dress their dolls to mirror their own interests and activities, such as pony riding, playing tennis or swimming and sunning.

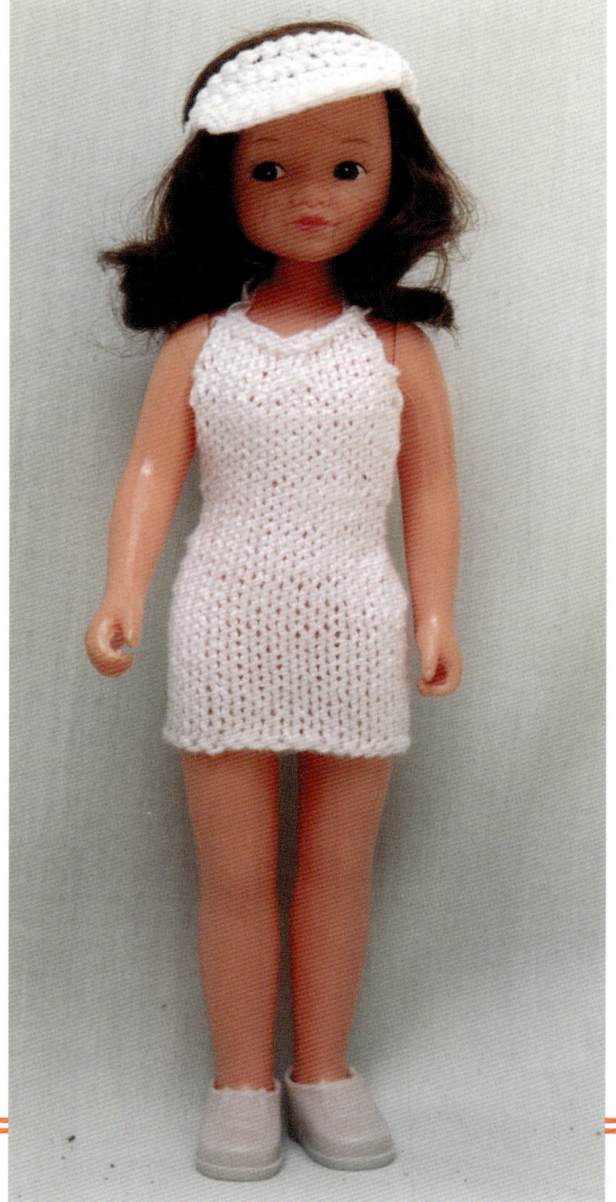

***Knitted and Crocheted Three-Piece Pony Club Outfit

Jacinda

7½ inches (19 cm) high

Dressed in a knitted mock-cable sweater, knitted jodhpurs and crocheted peaked cap, 7½-inch Riley by Kish & Company is ready for her first riding lesson. Patterns for the sweater, jodhpurs and cap follow.

Sweater

Materials

1 ball Sullivan or Milford soft knitting cotton (equal to 4 ply) or equivalent

#0 US (2 00 mm) [14] knitting needles

2 #4/0 (000 or 5 mm) snaps

Measurements

Length from shoulder to hem	2¾ inches (7 cm)
Width around at underarm	5 inches (12.5 cm)
Length of sleeve seam (cuff down)	1¾ inches (4.5 cm)

Tension

10 sts = 1 inch (2.5 cm)

13 rows = 1 inch (2.5 cm)

Abbreviation Note:

Twist: knit into front of 2nd st on left-hand needle, then into front of first st on needle.

Sweater

Instructions

Front

Cast on 24 sts

Knit 4 rows in k1, p1 rib

Pattern

1st row: k5, p1, twist2, p1, k1, p1, twist2, p1, k1, p1, twist2, p1, k5

2nd row: purl

Repeat these 2 rows 8 times

Armhole Shaping

Cast off 3 sts at beg of next 2 rows

Work 8 rows in pattern

Neck Shaping: First Side

Work 7 sts in pattern, turn

Next row: p2 tog, purl to end row

Next row: work in pattern

Repeat last 2 rows 1 time

Cast off remaining sts

Neck Shaping: Second Side

Rejoin yarn to base of neck, cast off 4 sts, work the remaining 7 sts in pattern

1st row: purl to last 2 sts, p2 tog

2nd row: work in pattern

Repeat last 2 rows 1 time

Cast off remaining sts

Back

Cast on 24 st

Work 4 rows in k1, p1 rib

Work 18 rows in st.st

Armhole Shaping & Back Opening

Cast off 3 sts, k9, cast on 2 sts, turn

Next row: k2, purl 9

Work 9 rows in st.st, keeping the k2 border at back opening on each row

Neck Shaping: First Side

Cast off 5 sts, work to end

Knit 1 row

Next row: p2 tog, purl to end

Knit 1 row

Cast off remaining sts

Rejoin yarn at center back, cast on 2 sts, knit to end

Armhole Shaping

Cast off 3 sts, purl to end of row

Keeping the 2 st garter st border, work 8 rows in st.st

Neck Shaping: Second Side

Cast off 5 sts, knit to end

Purl 1 row

Next row: k2 tog, knit to end

Cast off remaining sts

Sleeves (make 2)

Cast on 16 sts

Work 4 rows in k1, p1 rib

1st row: inc in 1st st, k5, p1, twist2, p1, k5, inc in last st

2nd at all alternate rows: purl

3rd row: k7, p1, twist2, p1, k7

5th row: work as 3rd row

6th row: purl

7th row: continuing in pattern, inc 1 st at both ends of the row

Work 5 rows in pattern

13th row: work as 7th row

Work 5 rows in pattern

19th row: work as 7th row

Work 5 rows in pattern, beginning with a purl row

Sleeve Top Shaping

Cast off 2 sts at beginning of next 2 rows

K2 tog at both ends of next row, and following alternate rows until 10 sts remain on needle

Cast off remaining sts

Collar

*Pick up 34 sts evenly around neck, omitting the k2 border on the back openings

Work 6 rows in k1, p1, rib

Cast off loosely

Note: to make a higher turtleneck-type collar, work more rows before casting off.

To Make Up

Sew shoulder seams (before further sewing, it is wise and easier to knit the collar). Sew sleeves into position. Sew up sleeves and side seams. Sew snaps down back opening to close.

Jodhpurs

Materials

½ ball Sullivan or Milford soft knitting cotton (equal to 4 ply) or equivalent
#0 US (2 mm) [14] knitting needles
Short length of thin elastic

Measurements

Waist to hem	4 inches (10 cm)
Waist to hem along side seam	4¼ inches (11 cm)
Waist to crotch	1¾ inches (4.5 cm)
Width around at waist	4 inches (10 cm)

Tension

11sts = 1 inch (2.5 cm)
14 rows = 1 inch (2.5 cm)

Jodhpurs

Instructions

Right Leg

Starting at the waist, cast on 24 sts, and work 4 rows in k1, p1, rib
1st row: knit
2nd row: purl
3rd & 4th rows: k10, turn, sl.1, purl to end
5th & 6th rows: k12, turn, sl.1, purl to end ****
7th row: inc, k10, inc, inc, k10, inc (28 sts)
8th & every alternate row: purl
9th row: k13, inc, inc, k13 (30 sts)
11th row: inc, k13, inc, inc, k13, inc (34sts)
13th row: k16, inc, inc, k16 (36 sts)
15th row: inc, k16, inc, inc, k16, inc (40 sts)
17th row: k19, inc, inc, k19 (42 sts)
18th row: purl
19th row: knit
20th row: purl
Leg Shaping
k2 tog at beginning of next 4 rows (38 sts)
23rd row: k17, k2 tog, sl.1, k1, psso, k17 (36 sts)
24th row & all alternate rows: purl
25th row: sl.1, k1, psso, k14, k2 tog., sl.1, k1, psso, k14, k2 tog (32 sts)
27th row: k14, k2 tog, sl.1, k1, psso, k14 (30 sts)
29th row: sl.1, k1, psso, k11, k2 tog, sl.1, k1, psso, k11, k2 tog (26 sts)
31st row: k11, k2 tog, sl.1, k1, psso, k11 (24 sts)
33rd row: sl.1, k1, psso, k8, k2 tog, sl.1, k1, psso, k8, k2 tog (20 sts)
35th row: k8, k2 tog, sl.1, k1, psso, k8 (18 sts)
Work 14 rows in st.st, starting with a purl row
Cast off ****
Note: lengthen here if your doll has longer legs.

Left Leg

Cast on 24 sts and work 4 rows in k1, p1 rib
1st row: knit
2nd & 3rd rows: purl 10, turn, sl.1, k to end
4th & 5th rows: purl 12, turn, sl.1, k to end
6th row: purl
Work from **** to **** (7th to 35th) row as on right leg
Work 14 rows in st. st
Cast off

To Make Up

With wrong sides of work together, sew up center back and center front seams. Sew up leg seams. If necessary, thread thin elastic through waist to fit doll.

Crocheted Peaked Cap

Cap

Materials

Small ball of Milford knitting cotton or equivalent
#7 US (1.5 mm) crochet hook

Measurements

Crown to band	1 inch (2.5 cm)
Length of peak	½ inch (1.5 cm)
Width around band	4¾ inches (12 cm)

Abbreviation Note:

tr (treble): Wrap yarn over hook 2 times, insert in stitch, wrap yarn over hook, draw through stitch, *wrap yarn over hook, draw through 2 loops on hook*, repeat from * to * 2 times.

Instructions

Make 4 ch and join into a ring
1st round: 2 ch, 7 sc, join to top of first 2 ch
2nd round: 2 ch, * 2 sc in first sc, 1 sc into next sc, repeat from * to end of round, join with sl.st to top of 2 ch
3rd round: 2 ch, * 2 sc in next sc, 1 sc into of the each next 2 sc, repeat from * to end of round, join with a sl.st to top of 2 ch
4th round: 3 ch, *2 dc in first sc, 1 dc in each of the next 2 sc, repeat from * to end of round, join with a sl. st to top of 3 ch
5th round: 3 ch, *2 dc in first dc, 1 dc in each of the next 3 dc, repeat from * to end of round, join with a sl.st to top of 3 ch
6th round: 3 ch, *1 dc in each dc, repeat to end of row, join to top of 3 ch
Note: if your doll has a larger head, work 2 more rounds as follows.
7th round: 3 ch, *2 dc in first dc, 1 dc in each of the next 4 dc, repeat from * to end of round, join with a sl.st to top of 3 ch
8th round: 3 ch, *1 dc in each dc, repeat to end of row, join to top of 3 ch

Peak
9th round: sl.st. 5 sts, 1 sc in each of next 5 sts, 1 hdc in each of the next 2 sts, 1 dc in each of the next 3 sts, 1 tr in next 2 sts, 1 dc in next 3 sts, 1 hdc in next 2 sts, *** 1 sc in next 5 sts, sl. st to beg of row
Fasten off
If you want to have a firmer peak edge, instead of continuing as at ***, sl.st to next st, turn, and work 1 sc around peak to the beginning of the sc sts, sl.st to next st and fasten off.

*Knitted Tennis Dress with Crocheted Visor

Jacqueline

7 inches (18 cm) high

Ready for tennis in her smart halter-neck dress, 7-inch Amanda Jane keeps the sun from her eyes with a quick-to-make crocheted visor.

Materials

Small amount of DMC Petra No. 5

Small amount of DMC Babylo 10 or equivalent, for visor

#1 US (2.25 mm) [13] knitting needles

½ yard thin white ribbon (optional, for straps)

#7 US (1.5 mm) crochet hook

Measurements

Front bodice top to hem	3 inches (7.5 cm)
Back bodice to hem	2 inches (5 cm)
Width around at waist	3 inches (7.5 cm)
Width around at hem	3½ inches (9 cm)

Tension

10 sts = 1 inch (2.5 cm)

12 rows = 1 inch (2.5 cm)

Instructions

Dress

Using knitting needles and starting at the hem, cast on 32 sts.
Work 12 rows in st.st
(Note: the length to the waist can be altered by knitting more or less rows.)
Hip/Waist Shaping
13th row: k7, k2 tog, k14, k2 tog, k7
Work 5 rows in st.st, starting with a purl row
19th row: k7, k2 tog, k12, k2 tog, k7
Work 3 rows in st.st
23rd row: k7, inc in next st, k12, inc in next st, k7
Work 3 rows in st.st
27th row: k8, inc, k12, inc, k8
Back & Armhole Shaping
Starting with a purl row, cast off 6 sts at beg of next 2 rows, then k2 tog at both ends of next 3 rows
Front Bodice Shaping
1st row: k6, sl 2, k6
2nd row: p6, sl 2, p6
3rd row: k2 tog, k4, sl 2, k4, k2 tog
Cast off remaining sts

To Make Up

Sew up back seam. Either sew thin ribbon to serve as straps to both front bodice peaks and tie at back of neck, or cross the straps and sew to back of bodice. Or you may crochet two strings and attach as you would the ribbon.

Visor

Using #7 (1.5 mm) crochet hook and DMC Babylo 10, make 37 ch, turn, miss 2 ch, work 1 sc in each ch to end (35 ch)
1st row: sl 10, 1 sc in each of the next 15 sc, turn
2nd row: sl 3, 1 sc in each of the next 11 sc, turn
3rd row: sl.1, 1 sc in each of the next 9 sts, turn
4th row: 2 ch, 9 sc, turn
5th row: 3 ch, 9 dc, turn
6th row: 2 ch, 9 sc, turn
7th row: 1 sc, 1 hdc, 5 dc, 1 hdc, 1 sc, turn
8th row: 1 sc in 1st st, *2 sc in next, 1 sc in next, repeat from * to end of visor
Fasten off

To Finish

Join back seam. (Note: If you wish to make the visor for a doll with a larger head circumference, add a length of narrow ribbon to each end of visor and tie in a bow at back of head). Using fabric stiffener, mold band and peak into shape.

Jade

7½ inches (19 cm) high

The quick-to-make bikini is worn by a 7½-inch Riley by Kish & Company, but it can easily be worn by a taller doll, and even one with a larger chest or waist, simply by adding 2 ties at each side of the panties, instead of the snaps.

Materials

Small amount of DMC Babylo 10 (or equivalent) in main color (MC)

Small amount of DMC Babylo 10 (or equivalent) in contrasting color (CC)

#8 US (1.25 mm) crochet hook

2 #4/0 (000 or 5 mm) snaps

Measurements

Top

Width around chest	4 inches (10 cm)
Length from top to bottom (widest part)	¾ inch (2 cm)

Panties

Length of side seam	¾ inch (2 cm)
Width of front waist (back similar)	2 inches (5 cm)

Tension

8 sc = 1 inch (2.5 cm)

Instructions

Top

Work 34 ch, turn, miss 2 ch

1st row: 32 sc, 2 ch, turn

2nd row: sl 8, 1 ch, 1 sc in each of the next 16 st, 2 ch, turn

3rd row: 1 sc in each of the first 3 sc, 1 hdc in each of the next 2 sts, 1 dc in each of the next 2 sts, 1 sc in each of the next 2 sts, 1 dc in each of the next 2 sts, 1 hdc in each each of the next 2 sts, 1 sc in each st to end, 2 ch, turn

4th row: miss 1 sc, 2 sc, 2 hdc, 2 dc, 2 sc, 2 dc, 2 hdc, 2 sc, 2 ch, turn

5th row: miss 1 sc, 2 sc, 1 hdc, 2 dc, 2 sc, 2 dc, 1 hdc, 2 sc, sl.st into next st

Fasten off

Edging

Miss the first 8 sc of original sc rows, join in contrasting color (CC), work 1 sc, 1 picot, *1 sc in next st, 1 sc, 1 picot, repeat from * to the last 8 sts of original row

Fasten off

Panties

Work 18 ch, miss 2 ch, turn

1st row: 16 sc, 1 ch, turn

Repeat last row 4 times

6th row: sl.st 4 sc, 8 sc, turn

7th row: dec, 4 sc, dec

8th row: 4 sc, 2 ch, turn

Repeat last row 8 times

17th row: inc, 2 sc, inc

18th row: inc, 4 sc, inc

19th row: inc, 6 sc, inc, 6 ch, turn

20th row: miss 2 ch, 1 sc in each ch, 8 sc, 6 ch, turn

21st row: miss 2 ch, 1 sc in each ch, 12 sc, 2 ch, turn

22nd row: 16 sc

Repeat last row 4 times

Fasten off

Trim

Using CC, work the edging as on the bikini top, around the leg opening and side seam

To Make Up

Top

Using CC, work 4 separate lengths of 32 ch—two to be attached for back ties, and two to be attached to front part of bikini to tie at back of neck.

Panties

Fasten each side with a snap, or if your doll is chubbier, make ties as per top, and fasten with ties on each side of panties.

*Knitted Swim Suit

Jaimie

8 to 9 inches (20 to 23 cm) high

Both variations of this knitted one-piece swimsuit are appealing: Version A is worn by a 9-inch wooden doll by Raikes Collectibles, while Version B is modeled by an 8-inch doll by the Alexander Doll Company.

Version A: 9-inch doll

Materials: Version A
1 ball DMC Perle No. 5 or ½ ball Pelicano No. 5 or equivalent yarn
#0 US (2 mm) [14] knitting needles
Thin ribbon in matching color

Materials: Version B
1 ball DMC Perle No. 5, or ½ ball Pelicano No. 5 or equivalent (navy or other MC)
Small amount DMC Perle No. 5 or Pelicano No. 5 in white or contrasting color (1CC)
Small amount DMC Perle No. 5 or Pelicano No. 5 in red or second contrasting color (2CC)
Thin ribbon in second contrasting color (2CC)

Measurements: Version A

Length from top of front to hem	3 inches (7.5 cm)
Width around at underarm	2 inches (5 cm)

Measurements: Version B

Length from top of front to hem	2½ inches (6.5 cm)
Width around at underarm	2 inches (5 cm)

Tension: Versions A & B
9 sts = 1 inch (2.5 cm)
11 rows = 1 inch (2.5cm)

Instructions

Starting at the hem cast on 34 sts

Version A: Work 14 rows in st.st

Version B: Work 10 rows in st.st

Waist Shaping

1st row: k8, k2 tog, k14, k2 tog, k8

Work 5 rows of st.st, starting with a purl row

7th row: k8, k2 tog, k12, k2 tog, k8

Work 3 rows in st. st

11th row: k8, inc in next st, k12, inc, k8

Work 3 rows in st. st

15th row: k9, inc, k12, inc, k9

16th & 17th rows: cast off 6 sts beg of each of these rows

18th, 19th & 20th rows: k2 tog at both ends of these 3 rows

Top Shaping

Version A

1st row: k7, sl 2, k7

2nd row: p7, sl 2, p7

3rd row: k2 tog, k5, sl 2, k5, k2 tog

4th row: p6, sl 2, p6

5th row: k2 tog, k4, sl 2, k4, k2 tog

6th row: p5, sl 2, p5

Cast off all sts

Version B

1st row: k7, sl 2, k7

2nd row: p7, sl 2, p7, break off main color (MC), join in 1CC

3rd row: k2 tog, k5, sl 2, k5, k2 tog

4th row: p6, sl 2, p6, break off 1CC, join in 2CC

5th row: k2 tog, k4, sl 2, k4, k2 tog

6th row: p5, sl 2, p5

Cast off all sts

To Make Up

Sew up back seam. Fold suit in half lengthwise, with back seam as one edge. Mark center of hem with a pin. Pick up 2 sts on each side of the pin, and work 5 rows in st st. Cast off. Sew cast-off edge to back hem, centering on back seam. Try swimsuit on doll, attach straps to peaks at front of bodice. The straps can either be tied at back of neck or attached to top of back.

Version B:
8-inch doll

About the Author

Marjory Fainges is the author of sixteen historical and reference books on dolls and toys, including six collections of knit and crochet patterns for doll clothing, such as *Classic Knits for Girl Dolls, Classic Knits for Boy Dolls* and *Classic Crochet for Baby Dolls*. The Australian-born author and her husband owned the Panaroos Playthings Doll & Toy Museum in an inner suburb of Brisbane from 1980 to 1989. A well-known lecturer on dolls and clothing in the United States as well as Australia and New Zealand, she is an active member of the United Federation of Doll Clubs (UFDC), for which she has served as Regional Director. She is currently a consultant on dolls and toys to the Queensland Musuem.

An avid doll collector, Mrs. Fainges learned to knit and crochet at an early age, first dressing her own dolls and, eventually, those of her two daughters. As well as designing her own patterns over the years, in the 1970s she began researching the history of dolls and their clothing, and in 1991 became especially interested in the history of knitted and crocheted dolls' clothing dating back to the late 1800s. She has since amassed an ever-growing collection of old patterns published in Australia, England, New Zealand and the United States. She has been married for more than fifty years and has five married children. More information on Mrs. Fainges can be found at her website: www.ozemail.com.au/~fainges.